JO OWEN
TRIBAL BUSINESS SCHOOL

with photographs and inspiration from Anthony Willoughby

JO OWEN

TRIBAL

BUSINESS

SCHOOL

LESSONS IN BUSINESS SURVIVAL AND SUCCESS FROM THE ULTIMATE SURVIVORS

JOSSEY-BASS
A Wiley Imprint
www.josseybass.com

Published by   John Wiley & Sons Ltd, The Atrium, Southern Gate, Chichester,
                      West Sussex PO19 8SQ, England

              Telephone   (+44) 1243 779777

Email (for orders and customer service enquiries): cs-books@wiley.co.uk
Visit our Home Page on www.wiley.com

Under the Jossey-Bass imprint, Jossey-Bass, 989 Market Street, San Francisco CA 94103-1741, USA
www.jossey-bass.com

Other Wiley Editorial Offices

John Wiley & Sons Inc., 111 River Street, Hoboken, NJ 07030, USA

Jossey-Bass, 989 Market Street, San Francisco, CA 94103-1741, USA

Wiley-VCH Verlag GmbH, Boschstr. 12, D-69469 Weinheim, Germany

John Wiley & Sons Australia Ltd, 42 McDougall Street, Milton, Queensland 4064, Australia

John Wiley & Sons (Asia) Pte Ltd, 2 Clementi Loop #02-01, Jin Xing Distripark, Singapore 129809

John Wiley & Sons Canada Ltd, 6045 Freemont Blvd, Mississauga, ONT, L5R 4J3, Canada

Wiley also publishes its books in a variety of electronic formats. Some content that appears in print may
not be available in electronic books.

Library of Congress Cataloging-in-Publication Data

Owen, Jo.
   Tribal business school : lessons in business survival and success from
the ultimate survivors / Jo Owen.
       p.   cm.
   Includes bibliographical references and index.
   ISBN 978-0-470-72781-2 (cloth : alk. paper)
   1.   Management. 2.   Business failures. 3.   Success in business. I.   Title.

   HD31.O8464 2008
   658.4'09–dc22

                                                            2008002735

British Library Cataloguing in Publication Data

A catalogue record for this book is available from the British Library

ISBN 978-0-470-72781-2 (HB)

Typeset in 9/13.5 Minion by Thomson Press, India
Printed and bound by Printer Trento, Italy

Contents

Introduction

Business is tougher than ever, and it is just about to get even tougher. Next time you go to the office, try the following exercise. Throw away your mobile phone. Throw away your computer. Dismiss all the consultants. While you are about it, get rid of all the HR staff, IT help desks, lawyers, brand police, supply chain managers and communications experts. Throw out all the paper: out go the budget reports, variance analyses and PowerPoint presentations. Now start leading.

To make the exercise a little more interesting, you will be given a special incentive scheme. Mess up and you will not lose your bonus or even your job. You may lose your life.

At this point, most sane managers will make their excuses and find something easier and more pleasant to do, like their tax return. However, for many leaders, this is not an exercise: this is their daily reality. Leaders in traditional societies do not have all the corporate life support systems that enable us and constrain us in equal measure. By stripping away all the complexity and sophistication of modern life, we can discover the essence of leadership.

The remaining traditional societies around the world survive in some of the planet's harshest environments. In the Arctic, the Saami herd reindeer from their winter pastures and the temperature can drop to −40 degrees Centigrade. In Africa, the Likipia have to walk five kilometres to fetch water in temperatures that rise above 40 degrees Centigrade. If the physical environment is harsh, the human environment is positively dangerous. The rule of law is precarious. In the highlands of Papua New Guinea we saw how tribal conflict led to burned villages, destroyed crops and dispersed population.

Despite the harsh environment and the lack of resources, many of these traditional societies have survived for hundreds of years. Few businesses survive that long. Less than 20 of the original 100 companies in the FTSE 100 survive after just 25 years. Entire industries have simply

Papua New Guinea: the elder liked pulling the feathers through his nose.

1

disappeared. Industrial Britain was built on coal and cotton; nowadays the only employment they provide is as heritage tourist sites.

If traditional societies can survive longer in harsher conditions and with fewer resources than modern organisations, then perhaps they are doing something right. Perhaps we can learn from them, instead of treating them as objects of charitable pity or as photo opportunities for cultural tourists. They deserve more respect than that.

For the last seven years we have been researching traditional societies to discover how they survive. If nothing else, such research makes you profoundly grateful for modern luxuries such as clean running water, hot and cold, on demand. The aim was to discover whether they shared in common any secrets of survival and success, and whether these lessons could be applied to modern organisations.

We did not approach the tribes as anthropologists. Anyone who has got near to anthropology will recognise that one of the most dangerous, divided and vicious tribes on earth is the tribe of anthropology experts: they all have their favourite theories, methods and tribes, which they protect and promote at all costs.

Instead, we approached the tribes as business people. We have worked with over 80 of the world's best, and one or two of the world's worst, organisations. We have worked in most industries across every continent except Antarctica. This gave us a reasonably good base of comparison. At the end of the research we have landed up respecting both the tribes and the businesses even more for the challenges they face and how they survive. We also discovered that tribes and businesses have much to learn from each other. The essence of that learning is condensed into this book.

Approaching tribes as business people made us unusual from the perspective of the tribes who hosted us. In Papua New Guinea they say that the only foreigners to go into the Highlands are Missionaries, Mercenaries or Madmen. We knew we were not missionaries, and we certainly were not mercenaries. That seemed to leave only one option. Perhaps it was an accurate description. We found we kept on asking dumb questions, like "What is important to you, what is your territory, what makes a good warrior/leader?" These things were so obvious to the tribal people it would be as if someone asked you how to use a tap to turn the water on. It is a tribute to our many hosts that they always treated us with great kindness. We were not treated as a potential

2

variance on their year end report: we were treated like human beings. Perhaps that is one of the first lessons of leadership: you lead through people, not reports.

There are plenty of reasons why we would not want to copy the tribal way completely. Poverty, disease, female circumcision, unpleasant male initiation rites, early death and a complete absence of MTV or espresso machines are just a few of the reasons. We may not want to copy, but we can learn about why they survive and how we succeed. Looking at traditional societies is a way of discovering and challenging our assumptions about survival and success.

Ultimately, this book is a journey in search of the alchemist's ultimate dream: the formula for survival and success.

Journeys of discovery

The harder we looked, the less we could see. Every tribe seemed to be completely different. The differences were obvious:

- Hunters versus farmers, traders or fishers
- Family groupings versus villages or towns
- Nomadic versus sedentary
- Territory based or occupation based

Even within the same ethnic group, there were huge differences. The reindeer herding Saami looked down on the fishing Saami; they in turn looked down on the Saami who had migrated to the towns. The Tuareg in Timbuktu still do the salt caravans to Mauretania occasionally; in Libya the Tuareg trade anything except salt.

Our fog of confusion was lifted by about 700 reindeer. They were migrating from the mountains down to the sea. It was about −20 degrees Centigrade and it was a miracle that they could survive by eating bits of lichen from the occasional black rock that protruded into the vast white desert of snow and ice. Somehow, they were perfectly adapted to the harsh Arctic environment. They had learned when and where to migrate to ensure their survival. Put the reindeer on to the plains of Africa, and they would not last a day: if the heat did not kill them, there would be plenty of predators happy to feast on such slow moving prey. Equally, put a lion, hippo or rhino into reindeer territory and it would soon perish. A lion in the Arctic is unlikely to be a happy lion.

❝ A lion in the arctic is unlikely to be a happy lion ❞

As with the animals, so with the tribes. There is no such thing as a universal formula for survival and success, just as there is no formula for the perfect animal or perfect predator. Instead of looking for perfection, look for fit. The challenge is not to be the best tribe, animal or business in the world. The challenge is to fit the environment in which you operate. The rules of survival and success change from tribe to tribe and from industry to industry.

As with most discoveries, it is a blinding flash of the obvious. Most of the fads that pass through the business tribe miss this reality completely. Each fad assumes that it is the universal solution to strategy, knowledge, efficiency or leadership. As with much that is obvious, many people cannot see it and fewer understand its implications. However, behind the diversity of survival formulas, there were a few common themes in terms of behaviour and organisation. These themes challenge many of the basic assumptions about how the business tribe should operate. This book will explore both the common themes and the different survival formulas for tribes and business around the world.

Five themes kept on re-emerging, from the highlands of Papua New Guinea to the middle of the Sahara:

- From competitive advantage to unfair competition
- From respect for the individual to respect for the community
- From the search for excellence to the search for fit
- From processes and procedures to principles and people
- From control to trust

From competitive advantage to unfair competition

The problem with a fair fight is that you might lose it. Tribal societies understand this well. If they lose, they die. In Papua New Guinea we saw the results of losing: burned houses, animals stolen, coffee crops burned down and the village dispersed. In Mali, we saw that loss can last for generations: on the outskirts of many villages you could find the Bella. They are more or less outcasts. They are descendants of slaves who were victims of Tuareg and Fulani slaving parties that terrorised the area into the twentieth century. For the corporate tribe the consequences are only slightly less dramatic: the loss of jobs as opposed to the loss of life and liberty.

Tribal societies recognise that if you have to fight, make sure that the fight is as unfair as possible. A competitive advantage over a wild lion or another tribe is too weak: they want to make sure that the lion or other tribe has no chance of winning. In the corporate world, such unfair fights would probably attract the attention of anti-trust lawyers, but in practice every successful organisation seeks more than a competitive advantage: they seek an unfair advantage. This chimes with Warren Buffet's belief in buying stocks in firms "which any fool can run, because some day some fool will run it". An organisation with a deep and unfair advantage is nearly foolproof.

The only way a business can achieve its target profitability is to have a few areas that achieve "excessive" profits to make up for all the other areas that are falling short, making losses or are investments for the future. Excessive profits come mainly from unfair competition, or from such benign market conditions that there is no competition. Unfair competitive advantage can come from many sources:

- Technology/patents (pharmaceuticals, software)
- Licensing (telcos, oil companies, etc.)
- Ownership of tangible assets (oil, property, utility companies)
- Ownership of intangible assets (brands, sporting rights for TV, Heathrow landing rights, franchise rights)
- Distribution control (pharmaceuticals, retail)
- Legal monopoly (central government civil service)

Most traditional sources of competitive advantage are weak: cost reduction, outsourcing, offshoring, process re-engineering and product innovation are all potential sources of advantage. However, equally smart and equally hard working competitors are going to be cutting costs at roughly the same rate. You therefore land up running faster and faster just to stay still compared to competition: the search for competitive advantage is often a recipe for competitive stalemate.

LEFT

Goat's blood tastes best when drunk fresh from the neck of the dying goat. At least, that's what he said… Kenya.

This list reveals another tribal secret: occupy territory where you do not have to fight at all. Traditional societies are not inherently violent or war like. They are smart enough to realise that the best way to survive is to occupy fertile, defensible territory that no one else can occupy. If your organisation can occupy fertile, defensible territory that no one else can occupy, you are likely to be in a highly secure organisation.

If you hear an executive talking about how they are seeking a competitive advantage, call your broker and sell the stock. Seeking competitive advantage means they are seeking a fair fight. As you think of your own organisation, answer three tribal questions:

- Do we occupy fertile, profitable market territory?
- Can we defend our territory, and with what?
- Do we have an unfair advantage, or do we risk fair competition?

FOLLOWING PAGES

The annual reindeer migration: going down to the Arctic for spring, Northern Norway.

These questions may seem naïve, but the simplest questions are often the best. The best answers are also normally very simple. The longer and more complicated the answers are to the above questions, the more worried you should become. Sophistication is the enemy of clarity.

From respect for the individual to respect for the community

"Respect for the individual" is a cliché that is trotted out with great regularity by executives who have been tasked with creating a corporate values statement. It sounds like a good value for our times: respect people regardless of their faith, sex or ethnicity; respect them by letting them have a reasonable work–life balance and by having family-friendly work practices. It is a value that is incomprehensible to traditional societies.

Traditional societies survive in some of the harshest environments on the planet. Their survival is a huge collective effort. Individuals can only survive if the community survives: community survival is the most important task for all individuals. In this environment, respect for the community is far more important than respect for the individual. The individual serves the community, rather than the community serving the individual. Serving the community well comes with the reward of greater recognition and greater responsibility. People are judged not by what they own and by what they take from society, but by what they give back to it.

The corporate tribe struggles to achieve much respect for its community. There are mission driven organisations in the faith, voluntary, public and military sectors where individuals are engaged *with* the organisation, not just *by* the organisation. They can achieve high performance with relatively modest pay scales. Profit driven organisations find it harder to create such a sense of mission and community. People may work very hard for an investment bank, but that is out of a deep commitment to themselves rather than to their employer. Organisations that have to focus on pay, working hours, terms and conditions to recruit and retain staff will struggle to create a sense of collective commitment to their organisation.

It is possible for the corporate tribe to create a sense of commitment to the community. Corporate organisations that have succeeded in this respect are often among the highest performing corporates. In Japan, although lifetime employment is fraying at the edges, there is a real sense of commitment from the organisation to the individual. In return, the individual is expected to show commitment to the organisation. The collective commitment stretches all the way down to individual sections of office workers: no one in the team will leave until everyone has finished their work. Peer group support and pressure is more compelling than another set of targets handed down from the planning group.

There are plenty of ways that organisations can create a sense of pride in the community that goes beyond pure personal interest. Organisations that achieve this are often among the highest performers:

- Give, and expect in return, high loyalty: Japanese companies in Japan
- Create an "esprit de corps", a belief that the organisation is special: some professional service firms such as McKinsey and Goldman Sachs

- Create a belief in a mission beyond profit: faith and voluntary groups achieve this, even Google with its "do no harm" motto reaches beyond the profit motive
- Create rich job satisfaction: the creative industries and politics are staffed with many people working very hard for very little, partly for the glamour and excitement and partly in the hope of hitting the jackpot and becoming a star

Traditional societies survive because individuals are totally committed to the survival of the community as a whole. Corporate tribes that create a sense of community, with people working not just for themselves but for something greater as well, tend to be high performing organisations.

From the search for excellence to the search for fit

It was festival time and no Dogon festival is complete without a fortune teller doing his rounds. He was a smart fortune teller: he promised me a great fortune in the future and then charged me a great fortune in the present. He would have made a good consultant or guru: he did not know what the question was, but he knew the answer and was prepared to charge a lot for it.

For as long as there has been management, there have been quack gurus selling quack cures to every management ailment. The medicine no longer comes in a bottle: it comes in a PowerPoint presentation, speech or training day complete with an accompanying book or video. Ever since *In Search of Excellence* was published over 25 years ago, quacks have been claiming to have found the alchemist's secret of business: how to convert average companies and leaders from good to great.

Tribes cannot afford the luxury of gurus telling them how to be excellent. They have to survive in wild, and wildly different, circumstances. From the golden sands of the Sahara Desert to the ice deserts of the Arctic they experience vastly different conditions. Some are nomadic herders, some are pastoral farmers, some are hunter gatherers. They may organise themselves into families, villages or whole regions. Searching for a universal formula for success is like trying to read smoke signals in the fog: it is an exercise in futility.

❝ *He did not know what the question was, but he knew the answer* ❞

9

The alchemist's formula for success in the traditional or corporate tribe does not exist and cannot exist when you think about it. If there was a formula for universal success or excellence, then everyone would apply it and the end result would be at best a competitive stalemate or at worst collective suicide: when everyone tries to do the same thing they destroy the opportunities for everyone else.

The solution, if there is one, is not excellence: it is fit. Each tribe has adapted the way it organises, the way it farms, hunts or herds, to the unique circumstances of its own territory. Where conditions are similar, there are similar solutions. The Mongolian steppe and northern Arctic do not sound similar, but in both places families are to be found following herds on annual migrations for the same reasons: both deal with harsh winters, mild summers and evil springs which can destroy the herd if winter makes a sudden reappearance and turns the spring pastures to ice.

This is good news for managers. Instead of management becoming as automated as a call centre in Bangalore, managers have to discover what works for them in their own unique circumstances.

From procedures and processes to principles and people

Hard as I looked, I never found the tribe's handbook for new tribal members. In most places, I found little paper and even less literacy. Tribes have to live on their oral traditions. When old people die, knowledge dies with them. Relying on oral knowledge has its drawbacks: try living for a week by relying on your memory for all your appointments and for all the phone numbers you need to call. In the absence of handbooks, procedures and processes, traditional societies have to find another way of managing their affairs.

Leadership is a contact sport. When Chief John invited us to his village, he had to explain it to everyone. He could not send out an email update, or wait for the next tribal newsletter. He told everyone the only way he knew how: he assembled everyone in the mud path that passed for Main Street

and told them. They then asked him and us many questions, and by the end of the session everyone not only knew what was happening, but they knew why it was happening, what they could do about it and they supported it by giving us a big welcome. Leaders should use whatever resources they can: strategists, coaches, consultants, committees and task forces all have their place. Ultimately, however, the corporate leaders are like tribal leaders: they have to lead people. In Kissinger's words: "Leadership means taking people, not like yourself, where they would not have got to by themselves."

Relying on oral knowledge also means that leaders cannot rely on rules and procedures. Weak leaders, and many petty officials, hide behind rules and procedures: rules become a substitute for thinking rather than an aid for thinking. Where there are no written rules and procedures, good judgement becomes essential. Even good judgement is not enough. The good outcome has to be achieved by a fair process. Fair process means that the outcome must be fair and that it must be seen to be fair, even by those who benefit least from the decision. Fair process takes time initially, but saves time later as the outcome is less likely to be sabotaged or challenged.

The larger the business, the larger is the corporate machine. It is tempting for the CEO to become the driver of the machine, focusing on the financial numbers, operating reports and strategic plans. The more effective CEOs recognise, like the tribal leaders, that they are leading people. Roosevelt, in the Second World War, said he was "just the traffic cop, getting people to go

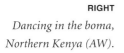

RIGHT
Dancing in the boma,
Northern Kenya (AW).

in the right direction". Success depends on building and directing a great team. For corporate and tribal leaders, the same rules apply:

- Focus on people, not processes
- Rely on judgement, not rules
- Achieve fair process, do not dictate

From control to trust

As part of the coming of age rites, young warriors are told to go off into the bush and fend for themselves until the rains return. This caused some problems when the rains failed for four years in a row. Sending them away for this time shows great faith and trust in young people. They cannot phone home every day or keep up to date with emails because they do not have phones or computers. In this respect, they are like every single leader before the twentieth century. Once they left sight of home, they were on their own and they were expected to perform. The people in head office cannot offer constant help: they simply had to trust that they had selected the right person for the right task.

66 *We live in an age of hyper-information and hyper-control* 99

We live in an age of hyper-information and hyper-control. This is not a question of Big Brother in government watching our every move: each time we surf the Internet, use a credit card or pass a security camera we tell the world a little bit more about ourselves. The real problem of hyper-control is in the workplace. We are in touch 24/7. Hyper-control works in different ways in different environments. Process driven environments, such as car factories and call centres, are able to monitor the performance of each activity to such a level of detail that they are becoming twenty-first century sweat shops.

Professionals cannot be controlled by processes in the same way, because the processes they follow have far too much variety within them. However, they still lack real authority. In flat, matrix organisations it is standard operating procedure for managers to have responsibilities that exceed their authority. This is hugely frustrating: it means that a large amount of time has to be devoted to building alliances and doing deals with colleagues to make things happen. Taking action requires a knowledge of how to work the decision making processes: getting the finance people on board, not offending the brand police, keeping HR quiet, paying off the IT people and making sure that no one in management sabotages your idea. This help is toxic to innovation: the easy life for all the staff types is to offer helpful analysis that identifies a few more challenges, risks and concerns. You do not get fired for identifying a risk: you can get fired for taking a risk and messing up.

66 *You do not get fired for identifying a risk: you can get fired for taking a risk* 99

As leaders, we learn to rely on our corporate life support systems: we need the information systems and the decision making systems that are the life blood of daily management. Tribal leaders do not have the luxury of such life support systems. Instead, they have to rely on people and to trust them to do the right thing. They do not control people through systems: control is exercised through peer group pressure and cultural conformity.

> **❝ *Corporate life support systems enable and imprison managers at the same time* ❞**

Corporate life support systems enable and imprison managers at the same time. At their best they create organisations that enable ordinary people to achieve extraordinary things. Too many organisations achieve the reverse: they control and manage extraordinary people into achieving ordinary outcomes. If we dare to learn from the tribal world we will recognise that everyone is extraordinary, and we will help them and trust them to achieve extraordinary things.

14

1. Strategy and Competition

Kill or cooperate

Traditional societies have not benefited from the wisdom of business schools, consultants and professors who have perfected the art of strategy. Perhaps that is why traditional societies are so good at strategy. They are not blinded by sophisticated analysis. They have not bought the book or listened to the inspirational speech. Tribes do not employ consultants to tell them how to think. Instead, they have to think for themselves. They have a high incentive to get it right: get it wrong and they may die.

❝ Tribes do not employ consultants to tell them how to think. Instead, they have to think for themselves ❞

Traditional societies that get it wrong collapse and go out of existence. Any traditional society that still exists must be doing something right in order to survive. As we searched through many traditional and business tribes around the world, three strategic themes kept on coming up:

1. Adapt to your territory (market)
2. Deal with the competition: kill or cooperate
3. Use your resources well

These are mind numbingly obvious conclusions. What is less obvious is how the traditional tribes do these things and how the business tribe can learn from them.

Adapt to your territory: the search for fit, not excellence

For tribes, geography is everything. The Great Wall of China is built along the line where the rainfall is about 20 centimetres a year. South of the Great Wall, there is enough rainfall for agriculture: that means settled people, villages, towns, standing armies and the rise of civilisation as we know it, from roads to road rage. North and west of the Great Wall there is not enough rainfall for settled agriculture. Farms give way to the steppe: look for as far as you can see, and you will see no roads, buildings, telephone wires or even fences: fences are the sign of private ownership which simply does not exist on the steppe. In summer, the steppe is a green ocean as far as the eye can see. This is the land of the nomad where they herd horses and sheep. This was the perfect breeding ground for Genghis Khan and the Mongol hordes.

The difference between the two sides of the Great Wall was caught in a friendship treaty in 198BC which says, "Let the state holding the bows beyond the Great Wall follow the rules of the Shanui, and let the Han govern the state of the overcoat and hat which lies inside the Great Wall." The initial shock was to discover that the Han defined civilisation over 2000 years ago by hats and overcoats (which could mean they would be disappointed with modern day New York or London). The second shock was to realise that rainfall dictated diplomacy: the rain starved parts of the world are rediscovering that rainfall drives diplomacy and conflict.

The two sides were divided by a wall, rainfall and different modes of survival. The two systems worked in their own environment: in context they fitted well. Neither system could claim to be perfect.

Each tribe adapts to its environment. In Mongolia, the land will not support farming, but it will support herds of sheep and horses who migrate on an annual cycle: individual families take responsibility for herding their own herds. In contrast, Papua New Guinea has rich land but the population is dense: organisation into villages that protect their territory makes sense. The Arctic, at first sight, appears completely different again. This is a harsh, barren environment where the land cannot support agriculture. However, it can support reindeer who migrate on an annual cycle between the coast and the mountains. Their environment is similar to the Mongolian steppe where temperatures can fall to −40 degrees Centigrade in winter. Perhaps not surprisingly, we find that the Saami in the Arctic traditionally organised themselves along family lines, in a similar fashion to the Mongols. Despite being separated by thousands of kilometres, similar environments gave rise to similar solutions.

FOLLOWING PAGES
Arburd Sands,
Mongolia: the weather
dominates all life.

BELOW
Anne Margrethe looking
after the herd.

In business, the search for excellence is a dead end. There is no universal concept of excellence: there is only what works in context. Look at the two lists of excellent American companies from around 1980 and spot the difference.

Excellent American companies A	Excellent American companies B
DEC	GE
Dana	FedEx
Wang	Coca Cola
Amoco	South West Airlines
Data General	Citigroup

The first, obvious, difference is that the A team no longer exists. These are the companies that were lionised and held up as models of excellence by Peters and Waterman of McKinsey in *In Search of Excellence.* They chose to define excellence only by looking at American companies, a myopia that exists in management literature to this day. The B list companies they ignored completely: they did not meet any of the rigorous selection standards they set for identifying excellent companies. Peters and Waterman successfully analysed what made large American organisations successful in the 1970s: not surprising that the formula has not worked in the next thirty years. The digital revolution, globalisation and the rise of Asia have changed the rules of the game out of all recognition.

In response to this change there has been an explosion of new management techniques: supply chain management, re-engineering, value innovation, TQM, balanced scorecard and Strategic Intent and Core Competences, to name a few. Some are useful, some are not. Managers have learned to surf all the fads. At some point, everyone has been through the same mill. A game for tired managers on a bad away day is to play the A–Z of fads (plus the one to ten). The rules are easy: first, name a tool or fad for every letter of the alphabet and for every number from one to seven. Then one member of the group calls out a letter and a number, and another member of the group has to explain why that alphanumeric combination of fads (like A7, Q3 or R4) offers the complete solution to the organisation's problems. You soon find that more or less any combination of fads can offer a plausible solution to more or less any organisation.

Tribal survival is not about fads. Fads blind us to the basic realities of survival. The essence of survival means having a secure source of food (or revenues) that you can defend against rivals (competitors) and that support the community (business).

The survival formula may be easy to state, but it is very hard to achieve. The formula works differently in different contexts. The people of the highlands of Papua New Guinea, the Tuareg in the Sahara, the Aborigines in Australia and the nomads in Mongolia all have their own unique survival formulas: they may not work in theory, but they do work in practice. As with the indigenous tribe, so with the corporate tribe: there is no universal success formula. There is only what works in practice. It is that which helps to make the task of management infinitely varied, frustrating and exciting.

Deal with the competition

Of the top 100 public companies in the UK 25 years ago, only 20 survive today. Many of the great and seemingly invincible giants of yesterday have disappeared. In endless industries, mighty giants have been felled by competitors who would not even have appeared on the radar screens of the giants of the past. Take a look at the list below.

Giants from 25 years ago	Upstarts over the last 25 years
GM, Ford and Chrysler	Toyota, Nissan, Honda
Pan Am, TWA, BA	Southwest Airlines, Ryanair
IBM, DEC	Lenovo, Dell
BBC, NBC, ABC	CNN, MTV
BT, AT&T	Vodafone, Verizon
Caterpillar	Komatsu

From Microsoft to Google and YouTube, new technology has created new industries and new giants.

Of course, there is an alternative to competition: cooperation. Cooperating with competition is a far safer way of securing success than competing. The problem with competition is that you might lose. Tribal people understand this principle well: they like to have friendly neighbours,

LEFT
Mongolian wrestling.

23

How to kill a lion: the art of unfair competition

To become a warrior, tradition holds that each cohort of aspiring young warriors must kill a lion. This sounds like a serious test of valour for anyone. I imagined young warriors taking on a lion single handed and bare fisted. If they tried that, they would indeed prove to be very brave. They would also prove to be very stupid and completely dead. So I asked them how they kill a lion.

As they patrol their territory, they see all sorts of wildlife. Occasionally, they will see a lion. If they are lucky, it is upwind of them, so it cannot smell them. Hopefully, it is still groaning, grunting and digesting a recent kill. It will be lying down thinking of nothing very much.

At this point, the young warriors will pull out a few arrows and dip them in some poison. Creeping up as close as they can to make sure they hit, they then shoot the arrows at the lion. Next, they run like crazy to the nearest cover they can find: the chances are that there is going to be a reasonably angry lion nearby looking for some retribution.

Provided they have all escaped, the young warriors now try to follow the lion at a safe distance. Eventually, it falls over and dies from the poison. Then the young warriors will creep cautiously up to it (just in case it is not really dead), cut its tail off and return to the village for some major celebrations.

None of this is remotely fair on the unfortunate lion. It is 100 % unfair. That is the whole point. The best sort of competition is unfair: a fair fight tends to be very costly and will as often be lost as it is won. There are some people who think that, in true Olympic spirit, taking part is more important than winning: this is patently not true of nuclear war or of business. The point is to make sure you win. Successful businesses always find some source of unfair advantage. Unfair advantage can come from technology and patents (pharmaceuticals and software); ownership of key supplies (oil and gas, film companies); distribution muscle (local utilities); government licences, protection and regulation (telecoms licenses) or from a carefully built up brand loyalty (fast moving consumer goods).

If your company talks about feeble "points of differentiation" or "competitive advantage" be afraid, very afraid: that is the language of an organisation that lacks the killer, unfair advantage. If you want to win, work for an organisation that has mastered the art of unfair competition.

not hostile neighbours. It is better to trade goods than it is to trade blows with each other. Normally, governments take a dim view of industrial cooperation, for the same reason that Adam Smith thought that business people should not cooperate: "People of the same trade seldom meet together, even for merriment and diversion, but the conversation ends in a conspiracy against the public" (*Wealth of Nations*, 1776).

" *The problem with competition is that you might lose* "

I first discovered the art of cooperation when working for a petrochemicals giant. They never referred to their competitors. They only referred to their "co-producers". It was a friendly and profitable industry at the time. In practice, rivals cooperate where possible. Industry associations are explicit cooperation forums that lobby government and manage the PR of the industry. Rivals even cooperate competitively, without any murmur from the anti-trust authorities. For instance, P&G and Unilever appear to be locked in mortal global combat in detergents and personal care products. Closer examination shows that in each category there is a market leader that normally also acts as the price leader. When the market leader puts up prices, everyone else duly follows. There is no need for pricing discussions at secret locations: the market etiquette is understood and followed by everyone. In airlines, you will find the same effect at work on business class fares which are remarkably similar for competing full service airlines on the same route. Competing on price would be possible (and etiquette allows for occasional and temporary price reductions), but it would be industry suicide. Any short term market share gains would be wiped out in an orgy of competitive price cutting which would benefit the consumers, but not the shareholders or the CEO's stock option plan.

Just as indigenous groups invest in having good neighbours, so too do corporate groups. The price of failing to invest in having good neighbours was clear in the highlands of Papua New Guinea: burned houses, destroyed crops and displaced people.

Camels, Christmas and cooperation

A camel was lost. It wandered to the nearest boma, or thorn fence that surrounds the small villages in the bush. One of the children inside the boma saw the camel and ran out to gather it in. This was like Christmas come early: a camel is worth serious money.

The elders gathered to decide what to do with the camel. From the markings on the camel, it looked like it came from a nearby village. With little hesitation they summoned the boy who had found the camel and told him to walk the camel back to the neighbouring village. The reasoning was simple: although they could have claimed the camel, the last thing they needed was to have neighbours with a grudge. You never know when their support might be needed. Returning the camel was a good way of ensuring they had good support from their neighbours.

Tribes, like managers, learn to pick their battles. Sun Tsu laid down three conditions for any battle to be worthwhile. They are as applicable to corporate battles as they were 2500 years ago:

- Only fight when there is a prize worth fighting for
- Only fight when you know you will win
- Only fight when there is no other way of gaining the prize

Most corporate battles fail at least one of these three conditions. In many cases, as with the camel, it is better to win a friend than to win an argument.

A quick glance at different industries and success stories show that the rules of corporate survival and success depend as much on their environment as they do for the tribes.

	Incumbent strategies: raise entry barriers and layer in advantages	New entrants: fight asymmetric battles
Customer focused	Branding and distribution: Pepsi, Coca Cola, Mars, McDonalds	Exploit white spaces (new territory): Sony, Whole Foods, WalMart, Starbucks
Competitively focused	Build network and scale economies: utility companies, Microsoft, Search engines	Exploit black holes and overlooked segments: Komatsu, Canon, Honda
Product focused	Internal innovation machines: pharmaceuticals, aerospace	Build a better mousetrap: Dyson, Freeplay, iPod
Efficiency focused	Learning curve, scale economies: chip makers, banks	Re-engineer costs: discount airlines, Dell

Even this map of strategic choices is simplistic: many companies shift the basis of competition over time, or mix and match advantages. The salient point is that there is no single source of competitive or strategic advantage, nor is there a single approach. If there was a single approach, everyone would home in on the same solution and the result would be a competitive stalemate and profit collapse. The frustration and the beauty of business is that there are an endless variety of solutions to an endlessly changing variety of challenges.

Use your resources well

Directing and using resources well is a central part of strategy: it drives everything from strategic plans through to budgets, rewards, measures and your bonus and promotion. Tribes also understand about resources. If they run out of key resources, like food and water, they starve. Maintaining good water flow is as important as maintaining good cash flow. Failure to do either leads to disaster.

In the tribal world, good use of resources means three things:

1. Find and protect your key resources
2. Waste nothing
3. Be creative in how you use limited resource

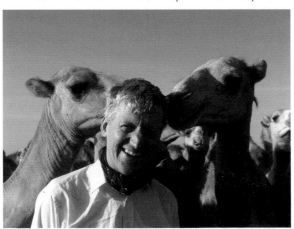

Finding and protecting key resources

When you live on the edge, you find that complexity and confusion are luxuries that you cannot afford. You need total clarity, focus and alignment:

- Clarity about the challenge
- Focus on what is important
- Alignment of everyone behind the same focus and clarity

The corporate world enjoys the sophisticated luxury of complexity, which does not help with clarity, focus or alignment. Different departments may have complete clarity and focus, but often on different things. This difference of focus and priority leads to endless low level internal corporate warfare. This warfare is unproductive for the individual but productive for the institution: internal competition is the way in which modern organisations decide where to invest limited resources and who to promote. It is a gruelling way of finding out where the best ideas and people are.

An oasis of common sense

I asked Ahmed to draw his world and what was important in it. He disappeared for a few minutes and came back with a simple black and white picture which represented part of the salt caravan from Mauretenia to Timbuktu.

I asked him what the scene at the top of the picture was. He looked at me as if I was stupid as he patiently explained: "You asked about my world: it is the salt caravan. You ask me what is important in it. We are in the Sahara Desert. I will tell you what is important in the desert: water. That is a well in an oasis."

That seemed fair enough. So I asked him about the scene at the bottom of the picture. Ahmed was even more direct in how he looked and spoke this time: "Bottom of picture? Sahara Desert. Oasis. Well. Well means water. That is what is important."

I looked at the picture a little harder. In the middle I saw what looked like four dead dogs with their legs sticking up in the air. I asked about them. Ahmed was now convinced that I was not just stupid, but mad. "Those," he said with a hint of exasperation in his voice, "are water bags. For carrying the water from the well. Across the desert. So now you know. When you live in the desert, the most important thing is water."

Sometimes, when we are locked in combat with other departments over projects, roles, bonuses, assignments, delivery dates and all the other standard corporate battles, it is easy to lose focus on what is really important. Corporate maps rarely have the clarity and focus that Ahmed achieved. What is the most important thing you must find and preserve in your corporate caravan?

Waste nothing

The corporate world is getting leaner and meaner every year. The corporate Olympics have one race, called "betterfastercheaper". It is a race that cannot be won. As soon as you get your nose in front of a competitor, another competitor appears with an improved version of betterfastercheaper. Everyone is running faster and faster (and better and cheaper). Although we are running faster than ever, we are in more or less the same position relative to competition. Like hamsters on a wheel, no matter how fast we run we seem to make no progress.

" *The corporate Olympics have one race, called betterfastercheaper* "

Despite this, the corporate world is full of luxuries that are beyond the wildest dreams of survivors on the edge: running water, air conditioning, comfy chairs, tea and coffee (sometimes even free tea and coffee), telephones and all the conveniences of modern life. Imagine for a moment what would happen if you got into the lift, pressed 6 for the sixth floor and found the doors opened out into the dusty bush of Northern Kenya. The doors shut behind you and you are left in baking heat.

Walk for a few hours through the baking heat and you reach a form of civilisation: a dusty strip of road with two or three shacks selling warm soft drinks. There was a school nearby with

RIGHT

Waste nothing. Bottle tops make a chequers board in Northern Kenya.

classrooms that had roofs but no walls and no books. However, there was plenty of hope: this was the place where futures were being built and dreams were coming to life. Outside, there were some bottle tops on the ground. Closer inspection showed that they were neatly arranged on an old piece of torn cardboard packaging. A child had drawn a chequers board on the cardboard. The face-up bottle tops were the white chequers, the face-down bottle tops were the black chequers. This was a place where nothing was left to waste.

Perhaps the bottle tops remind you just how thirsty and dusty you have become. Fortunately, the lift doors reappear, you step in and find yourself back in your office. The air conditioning cools you down, the water is clean from a tap, not brackish from a river five miles away, and you have all the books, internet and facilities you need.

The necessities we need are luxuries to others. When the pressures of the corporate Olympics become too much, take a moment to be grateful for the everyday luxuries that we can take for granted.

Be creative about how you use resources

Many years from now an archaeologist wandering through the remains of the industrial era will wonder what happened to all the mighty business empires that vanished as mysteriously as the dinosaurs. Entire industries simply disappeared. The original industrial revolution in the UK was built on coal, steel, shipbuilding and textiles. Those industries are now more or less extinct in the UK. The same industries transformed the agricultural mid west of America, first into its industrial heartland and then into its rust belt.

At their height, these industries appeared invincible. They had all the resources that any megalomaniac could wish for, and many megalomaniacs did run those industries: they were the "great malefactors of wealth" who were lambasted by President (Teddy) Roosevelt.

These business empires disappeared for two reasons:

- Their environment changed: being in a commodity business in a high cost country is not a good position when markets go global.
- Competitors became creative and changed the rules of the game. Ideas and creativity beat the dull weight of money every time.

" Creativity beats the dull weight of money every time "

The power of creativity over money is very clear in the tribal world, not least because they mainly exist outside the money economy. As you walk into the outback near Kununurra, in the heart of Australia, it is inconceivable that anyone can survive here. Credit cards and cash will not get you anywhere: there is nothing to buy. This is the world where original European explorers starved, while surrounded by food that the Aborigines would recognise and use. Whatever re-source advantages the Europeans had, they were useless in the wrong environment. Resources are only valuable if they are well used and you know where to find them.

The world's largest shop

Walking through the Australian bush, Jack invited me to spot the grocery store. I could see no buildings, only dust and bush. He then asked me to spot the pharmacy. If he could see a grocery store and a pharmacy, I thought he must be hallucinating or I must be going blind. Then he started tapping various trees and bushes and showing how they could be used as food or medicine. We were in the middle of the world's largest grocery store and pharmacy, but I had not been able to see it. We are always surrounded by resources, if we know where to find them and how to use them.

Each tribe showed highly creative use of minimal resources. Self-sufficiency means being able to use the local plants and animals for everything from transport, to food, clothing, containers and even housing. The warmth of the gers (tents) in Mongolia comes from having felt lining: each family makes its own felt from the wool of the sheep that it herds. The felt lining can also be used to make warm inner boots and coats. They are also experts at using dung effectively: it can be used for fuel, making walls, deterring mosquitoes in summer or insulating cows in winter from the intense, arctic cold. This is highly creative use of resources born of generations of experience.

Most businesses have to be sustained by large amounts of resource. Some industries, such as semi-conductors and consumer electronics, are on a never ending treadmill of innovation and big capital spending simply to keep pace with the competition. However, most businesses do not need vast amounts of resource to get going: they need vast amounts of creativity and commitment. If new entrants fight on the same terms as incumbents, they will be defeated by the weight of resource being used against them. Creativity is a far more valuable resource than money. Most of the successful dot.coms, from Dell to MySpace and beyond, have started in a bedroom or a garage.

LEFT

Mongolian ger (household tent) in morning fog.

When we started Teach First, we had more or less no money. We wanted to become a top graduate recruiter in the UK. Within five years, Teach First beat 97 % of the top 100 UK public companies in this market, despite being comprehensively outspent by organisations that have big brand names, large recruiting machines and well-established networks. The Teach First innovation was simple. Unlike most recruiters who like to brag about how wonderful they are (and they all tell the same story to increasingly cynical final year students), we made the radical decision to listen to what the students really wanted after graduating. We then tailored our offering to what they wanted and started talking about them, not us. Very little money went far with a little creativity and high commitment from all the staff.

Many organisations struggle to get out of the resource trap. If a group has a $2 million operating budget, the discussion is anchored around $2 million. The budget owner will try to raise the budget, others will try to cut the budget. In practice, the best predictor of next year's budget is this year's budget plus a bit for inflation, if you are lucky. Everything is geared to fine tuning the $2 million machine. No one asks if we need the $10 million machine, or perhaps a $100,000 machine instead. Organisations become trapped by their past.

Escaping the resource trap requires challenging the machine, challenging the basic assumptions on which we work. Teach First challenged the basic way recruiters recruited. Dell challenged the way computers were made and sold with the most radical of re-engineering approaches. The traditional computer manufacturer had a process that can be simplified down to two steps:

1. Make computers
2. Sell computers (we hope)

This is a nightmare process: it requires great demand forecasting, and hence market sizing and competitive analysis. Get it wrong and either you are left with mountains of unsold stock, huge discounting and a major cash flow problem, or you cannot meet demand and forego huge sales and profits. Within the resource trap mindset, each department strives to forecast demand more accurately, market more effectively to shift stock and to reduce the cycle time of the supply chain to minimise inventory. No matter how well you manage the process, it is still a bad process and will yield bad results. It is a huge waste of management time and talent.

Michael Dell had no resources when he started, so he never fell into the resource trap. He was forced to come up with a new process that can also be simplified down to two steps:

1. Sell computers
2. Make them

With that one change, all the problems of forecasting market demand, inventory management, stock-outs, fire sales and cash flow crises largely evaporated. If you have already been paid for a

computer you have not yet made, you are unlikely to have a problem with cash flow or unsold inventory.

Conclusions

Many organisations become victims of history: they are prisoners of success. Once they find a formula for survival, they rightly stick to it. This makes them very vulnerable to change: either the environment changes (steel and cars in the US rust belt) or the competition changes the rules of the game (the rise of Japanese consumer electronics companies). Few legacy organisations survive a fundamental shift of environment or competition. This means that the search for the universal formula for success is like the search for the alchemist's formula for turning base metals into gold: it is a search that is doomed to failure. There is no universal formula for success or survival. This is an obvious point which is completely missed by eminent professors of strategy and highly paid consultants and gurus who tout their latest formula.

If there was a universal formula for success, management would be very boring. Everyone would be required to apply the same formula and there would be little by way of innovation, creativity or change. If everyone applied the same formula, at best you would have competitive stalemate; at worst you have collective suicide as all the competitors attempt to do the same thing at the same time.

As with businesses, so with tribes. We did not find a universal formula for survival and success. Instead, we found that each tribe adapted to the unique conditions of its environment: pastoralists, hunters, nomads all had their own way of life adapted to their own environment. In strategic terms, their survival depends on answering three questions successfully:

- What is our territory/environment and how do we adapt to it?
- How will we deal with the competition?
- What are our resources and how can we best use them?

If your organisation can answer these three questions successfully, it is on the way to success.

2. Change

Change or die

If survival and success depend on being well adapted to the environment, then there is a very obvious consequence: when the environment changes, you have to change with it. Businesses are familiar with the challenge of constant change: new technology, new competition and globalisation all require businesses to keep on changing. Businesses find that they are running faster and faster to stay still. The faster they run, the faster the competition run. All the competitors run faster and faster, but relative to one another they stay still, or advance or fall back a little.

In contrast, traditional societies would seem to be islands of stability in a boiling ocean of change. Tribes may be traditional, but they are not fossilised. They are facing the need to change as much as anyone else. For them, change is not about staying in business. Tribal change is about staying alive. The pressures for change are similar to business. Change is forced on tribes by competition, globalisation and the changing environment.

Tribal change can be at least as radical and as fast as change in the corporate community. In the story of Shillingi (see page 36) the Likipia realised that they had to move from killing animals to tending and caring for wild animals. That is a 100 % change in direction. This radical change was brought on by four years of drought and incipient starvation. They realised that they were running out of animals. They needed another source of income, and realised that tourists were their best bet, but tourists wanted to see wild animals, not empty bush. So they stopped killing the wild animals and started protecting them. They got into the business of farming tourists instead of hunting animals.

OPPOSITE

The welcoming party,
Papua New Guinea.

Part of Shillingi's life map: a complete bloodbath.

Shillingi's story

Shillingi sat down and drew his life story. He was known as Shillingi because he had taken the King's shilling (and the King's boots and uniforms) when he signed up for the colonial army. Having got his hands on the goodies, he duly evaporated into the bush with his shilling, boots and uniform. He had clearly been an entrepreneurial sort of person in his youth.

As with all old men, he was given to a little embellishment. He claimed to have been born in 1868. Looking at his drawn autobiography, it was a bloodbath. When not raiding other tribes for their cattle, he was hunting elephants, lions and all the wildlife in the bush. There were endless stories of extreme hardship and even greater heroism.

On the final page of his autobiography, the bloodbath suddenly stopped. Where he had been slaughtering wildlife, he was now proudly conserving wildlife. This, by the standards of most corporate change programmes, is a fairly dramatic change of direction. We asked what the transformation was all about. "Simple," he replied. "Four years of drought meant that everything was dying anyway. We could not survive by hunting anymore. Our only chance was to preserve wildlife in the hope that this might attract tourists, so we can make some money and live."

If the environment does not change, then there is little pressure for tribes or businesses to change. However, the environment is always changing: the only question is "how fast?". When the world changes, we have to change to survive and to succeed: this is a truism that people recognise intellectually, but fight emotionally. No one likes giving up what they currently do successfully in favour of an unknown future. Like Shillingi, we have to learn to adapt, however old we are.

Wherever we looked, we found that traditional societies were societies in transition. Some are dealing with change successfully. Some are failing with terrible consequences for their communities. Behind all the differences between the tribes, we found some consistent patterns of success and failure. They were the same patterns of success and failure that change in the business community enjoys. Success or failure depended on answering four questions successfully:

- Is there a real need to change?
  — Where is the pain and who is feeling it?
- Do they know where the change will take them?
  — Who will lose (oppose change) and gain (support change)?
- Who is making the change?
  — Will people feel in control or at risk?
- Do they understand the costs and risks of change?
  — Will the benefits outweigh the costs and risks of change or of doing nothing?

These are the same four questions that businesses need to ask themselves before embarking on change. With tedious regularity these questions are neither asked nor answered properly before starting. With equally predictable regularity most change programmes fail to live up to their early expectations as a result.

Is there a real need to change?

Most normal people do not like change. Tribal people are normal people. Like normal people, they recognise that change means risk, uncertainty and doubt. If you are living on the edge, you do not want to take risks: taking risks may mean risking your life if your crops or food supply fail as a result of some imaginative risk you have taken. Within businesses, most staff do not enjoy change. If you have worked out how to survive in your current job you will not fall over in delight when a consultant tells you that your role, boss, performance expectations and compensation are all going to change so that the business and the CEO's stock options can enjoy a brighter future. Unlike normal people, CEOs and consultants enjoy change: they are able to control it and benefit from it.

Shillingi and the Likipia had no real choice. They had to change or face the prospect of starvation. That is a compelling need to change. A compelling need to change does not relate to some abstract corporate goal: a compelling need to change is personal. If the idea of doing what we are doing today has to be unacceptable compared with any other alternative, then people are prepared to go through the pain and upheaval of change. In the business tribe, change is often dealt with as an abstract idea and pursued as a technical project. Change initiatives fail with tedious regularity as a result. Successful change starts and finishes with people, and deals with all the politics and emotion which that involves.

Do they know where the change will take them?

There is little point in starting a journey unless you are going somewhere worthwhile. If you are living in a mud hut with no electricity, water or health care it is pretty easy to see that things could be better, especially when tourists start arriving in air conditioned buses with their video cameras to start recording what they see as picturesque poverty. In truth, poverty is never picturesque.

Wandering round the boma, I asked each family what they wanted for their village. With tedious regularity, they all gave the same answer: education, health and water. This was a positive vision that went far beyond the need to survive the drought. They always gave the answer in the same way: education first, health second and water third. This was surprising. The boma was about five miles from the nearest water source, and all the water had to be carried in buckets from the river to the boma. In temperatures that can reach 40 degrees Centigrade, this is hard work. My lazy view of the world would be to get the water sorted out first and end all the walking to and from the river. The tribal view was that an educated person never goes hungry: investing in the education of their children was the best investment they could make in the future of the tribe. Second, they needed to make sure their children stayed healthy. Finally, sorting out the water would give them the luxury of fewer walks to the river.

RIGHT
Lasse Mahtte: the only sleep possible is for a few minutes on the back of the snowmobile, otherwise the herd will scatter.

The Saami reindeer herders also saw that things could be better for them. Herding used to be done on foot with snow shoes, using a domesticated reindeer to pull supplies. If your idea of fun is to walk non-stop for 48 hours through temperatures hitting −40 degrees centigrade, then you might not see the need to change. Otherwise, the first sight of a snowmobile and you will quickly see how your life could be transformed. Even on a snowmobile, it is hard work. Within fifteen minutes the herd can scatter completely across the Arctic wilderness. At best, the Saami herders might get a few minutes sleep on the back of the snowmobile, while they wait for the herd to start moving again.

The Saami have now fully entered the cash economy. Many of them live dual lives. Most of the time they live in typical Nordic houses: warm with lots of natural wood and a sauna in the house. Nearby they will have a traditional tent in which they entertain occasionally. The tent may be traditional, but the house has central heating. That makes it an easy decision about where to eat, cook and sleep.

The Saami and the Likipia are in profoundly different circumstances, but both have a compelling vision of how they can create a better future for themselves. The need to escape a challenging past is mirrored by the idea of what an exciting future might look like. In both cases, the vision is personal. It is not about how some faceless corporate entity will be able to meet its profit forecast better. The vision of change is one in which each person can see how they will benefit.

Where you have both a compelling need to escape the present and a clear vision of what a better future looks like, you have a real chance of making successful change. On the other side of the world from the Saami, the Aborigines near Kununurra had both the need for change and a positive vision of the future, as in Dan's story (below). The circumstances may change dramatically from Africa to the Arctic to Australia, but the conditions for change are constant.

Many corporate change programmes focus on the rational world of enhancing earnings and reducing cycle times, defects or headcount. These are all important things to focus on,

LEFT

Britte's cooking set us up for the rigours of the reindeer migration.

but this focus also misses the point completely when it comes to making sure that the change will actually be implemented and succeed. They forget that change is about people, not projects. The CEO will get on to the website, do the roadshow and issue the news letter extolling the virtues of the latest change programme. After six months of tirelessly communicating the brave new world it is common to find a very frustrated CEO complaining that the staff just "do not get it" and that they are "change resistant". This then leads to a redoubling of effort, or firing people who are obstructive. The problem is not that staff "do not get it".

" *Change is about people, not projects* "

The problem is that the CEO does not get it. The CEO needs to translate the corporate agenda into something that each individual can understand and can see what it means for them personally. People see the benefits and risks of change from a personal perspective: effective CEOs know how to tap into that.

Do they understand the costs and risks of change?

Change is full of unintended consequences, because the future is inherently unpredictable. Traditional societies struggle with this as much as modern organisations.

Snowmobiles clearly make life easier if you have to herd reindeer through the Arctic. They also mean that the Saami have fully entered the cash economy. Suddenly they are having to deal with government, regulations, subsidies (hopefully) and planning disputes over windmills, holiday cottages and pipelines, which can destroy the traditional migration paths of their reindeer. They are, perhaps, more fortunate than their Saami neighbours to the south, in Finland. The Finnish Saami enjoy the support of the EU who have put up fences to denote the border with Norway and the border between properties within Finland. The problem with this is that migrating reindeer are not quite up to date with property law and do not recognise the value of fences. Migrating patterns have had to be abandoned and alternative ways of caring for the reindeer have been created.

The Likipia saw that the move from killing animals to farming tourists would cause upheaval. They accurately predicted that it could pose a major threat to their culture and to their way of life. They therefore appointed one of their elders, Daniel, as the keeper of the culture. He would also act as the interface with the outside world: they wanted to avoid too much cultural pollution from the tourists. After a while, they saw that Daniel had moved out of the boma and was constructing a concrete house. To Western eyes, it did not look like much; to local eyes, it was a palace. Among other things, it was going to have running water. Daniel was soon to be seen on a motorbike which he had bought for himself. There was even talk of a car appearing. All of this was justified on the basis that he needed this to deal with the outside world and to keep the cultural pollution away from the tribe. Meanwhile, questions were being asked about where all the money was going: was it going to education, health and water or was it going to motorbikes and concrete houses? The tribe had never faced the challenge of dealing with even modest wealth. It was at the start of a difficult learning journey.

Not all change is planned. Occasionally, it creeps up unexpectedly. Walking through one Dogon village I noticed that there was no litter. In many poorer countries, discarded plastic bags disfigure the landscape, but not in this village. People were too poor to have a shop, too poor to have plastic bags. They were, on the other hand, totally self-sufficient. They lived hard lives which may have been poor economically, but they were rich socially. In amidst this grinding economic poverty there was one unusual sight. The village had been given a black and white television set and a portable generator. Over seventy children were gathered round it. They were transfixed by a TV show in which rich kids in their best clothes were entertained in the capital, Bamako. The attractions of public circumcision and working all day in the fields started to wane in the face of such affluence.

As with the traditional tribe, so with the modern organisation. It is very easy to focus on the benefits of change and conveniently forget some of the costs of change. Introducing corporate practices into education, health care, policing and public services sounds like a good way of improving efficiency and accountability. It is also a good way of eroding the public service ethos

of fairness, service and efficiency. Playing games to meet government targets becomes more important than delivering the core service.

Who is making the change?

Here, for once, the corporate and tribal ways part company. In the corporate world, major change is normally driven from the top down. Change from the bottom tends to be incremental change: quality improvements and kaizen type activities on a car factory floor would be typical of bottom up change. Changing the type of car produced and the factory where the car is produced comes from the top, not the bottom. Driving major corporate change from the top is natural. The top of the organisation has the resources to make change, the political power to overcome obstacles to change and the oversight to make the trade-offs between competing priorities for limited management time and money. The dark side of top down change is that staff often feel disempowered, threatened and resentful of such change.

When the corporate way is applied to traditional societies, disaster follows. In Norway, after the War, the government decided to help the Saami. They needed help. The Germans had withdrawn from northern Norway burning everything as they left. Having no houses, no shelter and no food is not a good way to face an Arctic winter. The government decided to take the opportunity to turn the Saami into model citizens. For a long time, they had been regarded as drunks, layabouts, idlers, thieves, cheats and worse: it was thinly disguised racism. To help the Saami, they created special boarding schools for Saami children, where they could learn civilised Norwegian ways. Perhaps inevitably, the schools became home to terrible abuse which make grown men weep to this day. The children learned nothing positive about modern civilisation and were cut off from traditional civilisation. They became a lost generation.

Where tribal change has worked, it has been driven from the bottom up. Change has been by and for the people: each individual can see how change will benefit them personally. The Likipia are changing because they can see how it will lead to education, health and water. Lars Matthis, the Saami reindeer herder, has embraced the modern economy fully in order to support his traditional way of life as a reindeer herder.

Perhaps in the old world of command and control organisations it was possible to order change from the top. Mill workers in the industrial revolution did not have much of a say in how the mill was run. However, modern organisations are flatter: managers normally find that their responsibilities are far greater than their authority. The only way they can get things done is by engaging the support of their peers and colleagues. They cannot command their peers: they have to persuade them.

We are perhaps returning to the tribal tradition where change is not done by the leader to the community: it is done by and for the community. That makes the leadership task far harder. No longer is it possible for the leader to live purely in the rational world and to issue orders based on logic. Business leaders, like tribal leaders, have to engage hearts and minds. They have to deal with the people, not just the project.

The lost generations

The road to hell is paved with good intentions, and there were plenty of good intentions. The idea was simple: help the children of mixed European–Aborigine descent become fully integrated into European society. This called for some drastic action. Children were to be taken away from their mothers at the age of five and sent to missionary schools to get a European education. (This was the same solution applied at the same time to the Saami, half a planet away in the Arctic.) They would be given new names so that they could make a complete break with the past. At age 15 they would be given work: the girls would go into domestic service and the boys would become stockmen working on cattle stations.

As with the Saami, the same solution created the same problems. Many missions became homes to abuse. The children became outcasts: they lost the law, language and land that were at the heart of traditional culture. Nor were they accepted into modern culture: they had to get a passbook to go to a bar. Not many were given passbooks. They were given separate seating areas in cinemas, were served last in shops and could only be employed by employers with special licences. They even had to get permission to get married.

Eventually, the government decided to put things right. It scrapped the apartheid regulations imposed on the lost generation and insisted that they all get paid a proper wage, instead of being used as free labour by the missions and cattle stations. The missions therefore closed down and the cattle stations used helicopters instead of stockmen, who were all put out of jobs. Things did not get better; they got worse. At least the old system gave them jobs and self respect. Now they only had the dole to look forward to.

The results of these policies are clear on the streets of Kununurra where the drunk and the dispossessed while away their time in any shade they can find. Unemployment and welfare dependency have become an intergenerational reality; the Aborigines have lost their traditional culture and have gained little from modern culture.

Change is always hazardous. Destroying what you have is easy; creating something new is much harder. Doing change to people rather than with people increases the hazards of change dramatically. If the result is getting stuck halfway between two systems, the result is disaster. If you change, take the people with you and make sure you can go all the way to a worthwhile destination.

Conclusions

"To see what is in front of your nose requires constant struggle" (George Orwell). Sometimes things are so obvious that we cannot see them at all, and so it is with change. It is very easy to get caught up in the mechanics and logic of change. In the business world I have seen a room full of consultants starting a change program by creating a risk log, issue log (ask them what the difference is), a meeting log, progress log, room log, attendance log, telephone log and master log. It was all logic, no progress – until the consultants were fired.

Missing from all the logs were people. If you want to make change, you have to make it through and with people. Even large systems projects that involve spending fortunes on new software and hardware depend critically on humanware: people will usually be required to change how they work if the new systems are going to deliver on their promises. Check how much time and effort is being invested in training and supporting the staff in your organisation to prepare them for the next great leap in systems performance. The chances are that the people are an afterthought on the systems programme.

To make successful change in your organisation ask yourself the four tribal change questions:

What is the need to change? Can the pressing corporate need for change be translated into a meaningful reason why the people in front of you need to change as well? How will you earn their support? If you cannot make the case, expect passive resistance to slow down your efforts.

Where are we going? Can you translate the wonders of increased profits or decreased costs and cycle time into relevant benefits for the people in front of you? What is in it for them, besides more hard work and uncertainty about what the future holds? What are we in danger of losing that we do not want to lose?

What are the costs and risks of change? Recognise that most of your staff are likely to be human beings: they have hopes and fears. Move beyond doing the dry risk analysis for the business and understand the costs and risks of change for the staff, who are not in control of the change. How can you manage the costs and risks of change for them?

Who is making the change? As a matter of corporate survival, you need the support of some senior managers to make change politically viable. However, in a world of flat structures and diffused responsibility you also need the support of colleagues and team members. You can no longer mandate change: you have to negotiate change and win hearts and minds. No tribal leader can change unless the community follows: managers cannot make change unless they have the active support of those around them.

The human side of change is so obvious that it is routinely ignored. Ignore it at your peril.

3. Leadership

Respect, responsibility, courage and contribution

Think, for a moment, of Genghis Khan and Mother Theresa. Both were very successful leaders. Now swap them around. Let Genghis Khan sort out the slums of Calcutta in his own unique way and watch Mother Theresa lead the Mongol hordes on the rampage across Asia. Most people find this an unlikely scene.

Leaders only succeed in context. Churchill was the greatest of wartime leaders. He was utterly useless in peacetime. He had to endure, by his own description, twenty "wilderness years" between the wars. Think of all the high and mighty CEOs who dominate the business press. As soon as they leave their business, they disappear into the irrelevance of committee and commission land. Out of context and without the support of their organisations, they become mere shadows of what they were.

By taking people out of their context we can find out if they are genuinely good leaders in their own right, or if they are simply successful creations of their own organisations. It is also how we can learn about leadership: by leading in different contexts we can discover if there are any universal rules of leadership, versus the particular rules of survival and success in our own organisation.

Tribal leaders, like business leaders, live in unique contexts. They lead without all the corporate life support systems that enable and constrain us at the same time. They are leading without a safety net. If leading a salt caravan across the Sahara requires any of the same skills as leading a project team in a media company, we may get close to discovering the essence of leadership. Before we set off in search of the essence of leadership, stop and think for a moment what you expect from a good leader.

Listen to the leadership gurus and you will probably hear that you have to be inspirational and charismatic. This is unhelpful to the 99.99 % of us who are not charismatic: I am not sure there is a charisma training course or a charisma transplant service available yet. You may also be told that you have to be some combination of Mahatma Ghandi, Genghis Khan, George Washington and Pericles all rolled into one. Some managers think they are at least that good already: they are normally well worth avoiding. We cannot succeed by trying to be someone else. Equally, we cannot succeed just by being ourselves and hoping, like a brooding teenager in full hormonal angst, that the world will recognise our innate brilliance and humanity.

Rather than speculate about what makes a good leader, we asked people in the corporate tribe what they wanted from their leader. Five themes emerged consistently:

- Vision
- Ability to motivate others
- Decisiveness
- Ability to handle crises
- Honesty and integrity

Before rushing off to see if the tribes have the same values, we should reflect on these simple findings. First, note the absence of charisma and inspiration: these are great qualities if you have them, but you can be a very good leader without them. Second, all the skills are more or less learnable skills: you do not have to be born to lead. This is what people meant about each skill:

Vision

This is not about copying Martin Luther King saying "I have a dream…." If you dream in the office, keep it to yourself. It is simpler than that. It is no more than saying: "This is where we are, this is where we are going, and this is how we are going to get there." To make it inspirational, you add two more elements: "This is why the goal is worthwhile and exciting to you, and this is the very important role you will play in helping us all get there." The B grade vision is about the organisation. An A starred grade is when that vision is made personal and relevant to each individual.

Ability to motivate others

This is where there was the greatest dissatisfaction with leaders. We found high motivation correlated strongly with positive answers to just three statements:

- My boss cares for me and my future
- I trust my boss
- I have a worthwhile job

Everything else paled into nonexistence: working hours, work–life balance, level of pay, recent bonuses and working conditions simply did not get a look in. Show you care for your team and you are in severe danger of being seen as a good and motivational boss. Do it really well and you run the risk of being seen as charismatic and inspirational.

Decisiveness

This speaks for itself. We found that although people always complain about their leaders, they enjoy being able to delegate upwards: let the boss deal with a problem and get the blame for the wrong solution. Most people dislike ambiguity: a good leader is able to blow away the cobwebs of uncertainty and provide clarity and direction where others see only chaos and confusion.

Ability to handle crises

In a crisis some people hide: analysts analyse everything and do nothing and some brave souls may offer some advice. It is at this point that the leader emerges, takes control and drives to action. Apathy, analysis and advice do not solve crises: action solves crises.

Honesty and integrity

This was the surprise entry into the top five. It was also the most divisive. Leaders who were rated low on honesty and integrity were trashed on all their other qualities as well: if you fail the honesty test, you fail every test. For leaders, honesty is not about morality. It is more important than that. It is about trust. No one wants to follow a leader they do not trust. An effective leader is a trusted leader.

The honest shark

The investment banking tribe exists in a very hostile environment: it is a shark pool. Therefore, when the suave investment banker sat down behind his fake antique desk and started to explain how important honesty was, I looked at him in goggle-eyed disbelief. Being smart as well as suave, he saw my incredulity.

"I may believe you," I said, dishonestly, "but no one else will believe your talk about honesty: you're an investment banker." Flattery was never my strongest suit.

The banker winced imperceptibly, and then carried on smoothly: "Honesty is nothing to do with ethics or morality," he declared, to my surprise. "It is much more important than that. It is about survival. If my team does not trust me, they will walk out across the road. There are plenty of people who would hire them today. If my clients do not trust me, I would have no clients. An investment banker with no clients and no team is no use."

"Building trust requires a strong form of honesty. Politicians have a weak form of honesty: they say they are honest provided they have not been found guilty of lying in a court of law. Leaders need the strong form of honesty: dealing with uncomfortable truths early on, not hiding awkward facts and not misleading people. That is the only way to build trust. No wonder no one trusts politicians with their weak form of honesty."

He looked satisfied with himself: he had identified a lower form of life than himself. However, being smart, he had also figured out an essential truth of leadership. Honesty is not about morality: it is about trust. Without trust, no leader can expect to have followers for very long.

Leadership in traditional societies

The starting point for leaders in traditional societies is fundamentally different from the starting point for leaders in the corporate world. In each traditional society we saw that the leader was either elected by the community or could be removed by the people if they were not doing a good job. Even where the leaders were traditionally drawn from a small group of families, there was still competition between potential leaders to prove themselves worthy of the trust of the people.

This sets the tribal leader apart from leaders in the corporate world, who tend to be appointed by obscure committees with even more obscure processes. In the tribal world, legitimacy comes from the people who will be led. In the corporate world, legitimacy comes from the appointments committee.

From these different starting points come different behaviours. In the business world leadership is often seen as something you do to the organisation and employees on behalf of shareholders. In the tribal world, leadership is something you do with and for the people on behalf of the community: you have to earn and maintain legitimacy from the people you lead every day.

From Papua New Guinea to the Sahara we found the same four themes emerging when people thought about what makes a good leader:

- Responsibility
- Respect
- Contribution
- Courage

Responsibility

Leadership in traditional societies is personal and visible. There is no hiding place, physically or emotionally. There are no committees to be blamed when things go wrong. The leaders recognise that they are totally accountable to their community. They do not have the option of disappearing off to another job or tribe when things go wrong; they can not disappear into a golden retirement if things go well. They live and die with the consequences of their own actions.

Respect

Tribal elders do not demand respect from others. The elders know that they have to earn respect. Respect comes from what you do, not from your position. Some senior managers miss this point completely. Earning respect requires acting as a role model, so that the younger generations can learn how to behave and how to earn respect for themselves.

Contribution

A successful leader is not judged by how much he takes out of the community, but by how much he gives back. At a highly practical level, this means helping out if a family runs into debt problems, supporting and promoting a local school or water project and improving the life of the community.

> ## The farmer's life
>
> The Bambara are the main farming tribe in Mali. The old farmer sat down and drew his life story. He explained it simply: "In the first twenty years of my life I was learning how to farm, what it meant to be a good Bambara. In the second twenty years I was taking responsibility for my farm and my family. The final twenty years of my life are about teaching the younger generation how to farm and what it means to be a good Bambara." For the Bambara, contribution to the community is at the centre of all three phases of their lives.

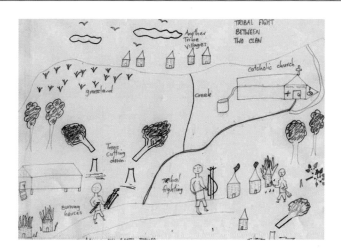

LEFT

Papua New Guinea territory map by a twelve year old: burned houses, destroyed crops. Tribal life is not idyllic.

Courage

In some societies, there is still a need for physical courage. In Papua New Guinea, when the children drew maps of their territory, they drew pictures of houses being burned down, crops destroyed and cash earning coffee bushes being cut down.

These are difficult memories for a twelve year old to have. More often, courage was about having the moral courage to take unpopular decisions and to carry the community with them. Being wise is nothing unless you can put the wisdom into action: that requires courage. Physical courage may not be the currency of the corporate tribe, but moral courage is. The good corporate leader needs courage to act decisively in crises and to take responsibility for the setbacks as well as for the successes.

" *Being wise is nothing, unless you can put the wisdom into action* **"**

Asking what makes a good leader is one thing: watching a leader in action is another. As we watched, all the tribal leaders displayed two more qualities which are so obvious that many corporate leaders manage to miss them. The tribal leaders we observed:

- Led by example
- Focused on people

Laughing at hyenas

I had been asking the locals what they expected of a good leader. They all gave the same reply: "Courage, contribution and responsibility." The reply was so consistent that I half expected to see little brass plaques, motivational posters and a video about courage, contribution and responsibility in each hut, but the huts had no water, electricity or even windows.

I felt a little cynical about this "courage, contribution and responsibility" mantra. It felt far too corporate. I decided to go for a walk and a talk with one of the warriors to see if I could discover the truth. As we walked through the bush I suddenly saw, from the left, a hyena sprinting towards us at top speed. In the fear of the moment the hyena seemed to me to be at least five metres high with jaws the size of a dinosaur. I instinctively did what any smart coward would do: I hid behind the warrior. The warrior might not save me, but at least he would die first and the hyena might then go away.

The warrior laughed in the face of imminent death, which struck me as one reason he was a warrior and I was not. The reason for the warrior's laughter quickly became clear. Immediately after the hyena appeared, a small boy brandishing an even smaller stick came hurtling out of the bush chasing the hyena. The boy was smaller than the hyena, but the hyena knew it had met its match. The boy was chasing the hyena, because he had been herding the family's goats. Given that goats represent the entire wealth of the family, this represents an impressive degree of delegation and trust to the junior members of the group. The boy showed that he deserved the trust. That one moment of mad bravery was an instinctive reaction born of years, of generations, of cultural indoctrination: you protect the herd at all costs.

The boy had given me all the answers I needed about courage, contribution and responsibility. By attacking the hyena with a small stick, he had shown plenty of courage. He had also made a great contribution by protecting the herd of goats, and he had taken responsibility for the situation: he had not waited for help from the warriors or formed a hyena management task force to work out what should be done by whom according to what timetable. By doing all of this, he had earned great respect for himself from his elders and from me.

Leadership values do not exist in words on plaques and posters. They exist only in actions. We understand the values of our organisations from who gets promoted, who gets the big bonus, who gets praised. Courage, contribution, responsibility and respect may not be the right values for leaders in every organisation, but they would be a good start:

- Courage to act on crises rather than analyse and advise
- Taking responsibility rather than shifting blame
- Contribution: focus on what you can give to the organisation, not just what you can get from it
- Earning respect by being a role model, rather than demanding respect

Leading by example

We went for a walk in the bush with Chief Warrior Kool and a few young warriors. As is the way with teenagers, the young warriors spent a fair amount of time fooling around on the fringes of the group. Kool ignored them. After a while, I began to notice that every time Kool found a piece of litter in the bush, he picked it up and packed it up. If there was a load to be shifted, he quietly shifted it. If there was an obstacle to be removed, he took the lead in removing it. After an hour or two, even the young warriors began to get the message. One of them saw a piece of litter and picked it up, slightly embarrassed. A huge grin swept across Kool's face and even the young warriors laughed. The day's lesson had been a success, without a word being said.

We saw similar things in other traditional societies. On the reindeer migration in the Arctic, it was the father who stayed up for 48 hours non-stop to keep the herd together. On the Tuareg salt caravan, it is the leader who takes the critical role — not at the front, but at the back of the caravan: here, he can see if any of the loads on the camels are slipping, or if any of the camels or Tuareg are suffering and need help.

All leaders set an example. Some examples are good and others are bad: think of Enron. Followers, employees, pick up the signals from their leaders as surely as the young warriors picked up the signals from Kool. Frequently, the example set by corporate leaders is the aspirational example: "If you work

TOP
Chief Kool, looking cool in the author's tie.

LEFT
Jump dancing, Laikipia (AW).

51

hard then you can land up like me with money, status and prestige." The allure of the trophy house and trophy spouse remains strong and people will make great personal sacrifices to get there.

An essential legacy of the leader is the culture she or he leaves behind. If the boss is a mean, Machiavellian miser do not expect the followers to be generous team workers. Leaders have a choice about what sort of example they want to set. Choose wisely.

Focus on people

Tribal leaders really have no choice here: they are not distracted by balance sheets, supply chains, strategy reports and IT systems. Their only resource is people. This makes leadership a contact sport for tribal leaders. They cannot motivate people by putting in a new compensation scheme, sending out motivational videos, hiring and firing to get the right kinds of people into the tribe. Leadership is up close and personal. When they need to persuade people, they do it in person. When they make decisions, they do it with the consent and support of the community, not by some high level committee which then communicates the decision by email. When there is a dispute to be settled, they do it in person instead of resorting to policy manuals and procedures administered by HR professionals working with advice from the legal team.

Most effective corporate leaders fully understand that they lead through people. The more senior people become, the more they focus on building the right team as a starting point for success. The real problems occur in the middle of organisations, where managers often feel so constrained by the corporate machine that they lose sight of the essential need to lead through people.

Leadership as a contact sport

Focus on people and leading by example means that leadership is a contact sport in traditional societies. They cannot lead by email, newsletter and strategic planning. They lead with and through people.

When we arrived at the Bari village in the highlands of Papua New Guinea, we were objects of great curiosity. Chief John had to find some way of explaining what was going on and getting the support of the village. He did so in the simplest way: he asked everyone to gather round while he explained what was happening. Two hundred people sat down and gathered round him. As soon as he stood up, they fell silent: he had a commanding presence. They hung on his every word and when he finished the flood gates were opened to questions. Two hours later the discussion was over and the fate of the pig was sealed: I went off to see it killed and prepared for the party that was to follow that night.

Persuasion happens best face to face, not through the sophisticated, high tech but impersonal corporate systems at the disposal of leaders in large organisations.

Living from the Stone Age to the space age

Sir Joseph Nomburi was born in the Stone Age. He remembered his astonishment the day a missionary came to the village. The missionary was clearly smart: he seemed to have answers to everything. The secret was his friend, the talking paper. Seeing the power of the talking paper, young Joseph decided he wanted a friend like that too, so he set about getting himself educated. The school he boarded at was a two day walk away, through hostile tribal territory.

His perseverance paid off. He eventually became a District Collector. At one point, resolving a tribal dispute involved climbing down a well to recover a tribal member, who was presumed to have been murdered. He had not been murdered: he got drunk and fell into the well. No one else had dared climb into the well: as a leader, and unmarried as well, Joseph elected to go down himself.

As he told the story, I thought back to the small boy attacking the hyena. Thousands of miles away in another culture, another young leader was showing exactly the same qualities of leadership:

- Courage: many thought climbing into the well was a one way trip
- Contribution: he stopped a deadly vendetta emerging between tribes
- Responsibility: he took the action which no one else dared to

Years later, he became Ambassador to the Imperial Court in Tokyo and received a well deserved knighthood from the Queen. In sixty years he claimed to have emerged from the Stone Age to the space age, but the qualities of the leader remained constant throughout the thousands of years he spanned.

LEFT

Sir Joseph Nomburi: lived from the Stone Age to the space age, Papua New Guinea.

How to avoid messing up as a leader

It is useful to know how to be a good leader. It is also useful to know how to mess up. Avoiding mistakes is as useful as scoring successes in the leadership stakes. In practice, there are countless creative ways in which people contrive to fail. Two contrasting themes came through strongly from corporate and indigenous tribes.

❝ *Avoiding mistakes is as useful as scoring successes in the leadership stakes* ❞

In the corporate tribe, lack of honesty and integrity in a leader is fatal. This is not about morality: it is about trust. When people do not trust their leader, they do not want to follow. Other failures, such as the ability to motivate and the lack of decisiveness or vision, are also important. However, they are qualities where no one is perfect and no one is completely beyond hope. Honesty and integrity are different: once the bond of trust is broken, the relationship with the leader is lost for good.

I asked Choidog, the Mongolian superstar horse trainer, if there was any unforgivable mistake for a leader to make. He thought about it. When I suggested honesty and integrity were important, he laughed: it was inconceivable that a leader could be dishonest and remain part of the community. Then he added: "There is one thing you should never do: never demean anyone. Never."

Choidog put his words into action. We watched a horse race in his honour. It was a 30 kilometre race with over 200 horses charging over the Mongolian steppe. It was like watching the Mongol hordes descending. The government had supplied a motorbike as the first prize, and one of Choidog's horses was strongly favoured to win. His horse led most of the way, until the saddle started

to come loose. The child jockey had to dismount and reaffix the saddle. Even with the halt, the horse nearly won at the line. Nearly is not enough to win a motorbike. Choidog could have criticised the jockey: the right procedure is, apparently, to let the saddle fall off and continue bare back. However, Choidog did not criticise and did not demean the jockey. He took responsibility himself: he should have double-checked the saddle and he should have trained and briefed the jockey on what to do. It would be easy to blame a 12 year old and tempting to do so when you have just lost a motorbike, but that would have achieved nothing beyond demeaning and disheartening the child. Choidog took the failure on his own shoulders instead.

It would be nice to think that corporate leaders and systems never demean their followers. A culture in which everyone is valued, trusted and respected for what they can achieve is likely to encourage the best in people. Corporate life is not always like that. Corporate followers are demeaned constantly in countless small ways:

- Status symbols, from office space to flowers and cars and perks, are a constant reminder of the pecking order. This soothes the egos of the people at the top, but demeans the rest
- Hyper-information and hyper-control send a simple message that staff cannot be trusted
- Many organisations are better at delegating blame than delegating praise
- Decision making hierarchies are efficient, and are an explicit way of excluding people from decisions that affect their lives. Consultation processes are often no more than token efforts, which further remind people how far they are from controlling their fate

Conclusions: lessons of leadership

There is no such thing as a universal formula for leadership. No one is perfect and no one gets ticks in all the boxes. If we find a context that plays to our strengths, we are on the way to success. Although there is no single formula for success, there are some consistent themes. In the corporate world, people look for five qualities in their leaders:

- Vision
- Ability to motivate others
- Ability to handle crises
- Decisiveness
- Honesty and integrity

In the tribal world the themes are perhaps less sophisticated and more direct:

- Courage
- Contribution
- Responsibility
- Respect

These qualities can only be demonstrated in action and in person: for the tribes leadership is a contact sport and it is about people. You cannot lead by sitting behind a desk. In dealing with people, trust is the positive virtue and demeaning people is the one vice to avoid.

❝ *You cannot lead by sitting behind a desk* ❞

We cannot all be charismatic super hero leaders. However, if we demonstrate courage, contribution, responsibility and respect we will at least be on the road to success.

4. Learning to Lead

Role models and the role of books and courses

Learning to lead

I decided to ask leaders of the corporate tribe what makes a good leader. After about six months of listening to leaders talking about themselves self-importantly, I realised I had been asking the wrong question. This is a painful discovery to make. The far more interesting question to ask is: "How did you learn to lead?" I gave all my interviewees six choices, from which they could pick two. Try it yourself:

- Books
- Courses
- Peers
- Bosses
- Role models
- Experience

The wholly predictable answer was that everyone chose some combination of learning from experience and learning from other people. Only one person chose books or courses: she was the only one who had not finished her formal education. This could be seriously bad news for someone who writes books and provides courses.

Not surprisingly, no one in any of the traditional societies chose books or courses either: there is a distinct lack of courses or books on "How to lead your tribe". As with the corporate world,

OPPOSITE
Timbuktu mosque.

they value experience greatly. The Dogon elect their spiritual leader explicitly from among the oldest males in the village.

Emphasis on experience can have some unexpected outcomes. In Papua New Guinea I asked Chief John who he wanted to become the next chief after he was gone. Chief John said it would be a democratic decision for the village to make. Then he added, with a laugh, "…and of course I expect my son to succeed, just as I succeeded my father." His reasoning was simple. "Every time there is a dispute to settle, people come to my house. My sons see and hear everything, even when they are babies. They are learning all the time what it takes to be a good leader. They are learning and remembering all the petty disputes and agreements which I have brokered. They are the living memory of all the decisions I have made. Why would the village choose anyone else to be their chief?"

By the end of his description, I was nearly converted to his elective-hereditary principle of leadership. His salient point, that experience helps leaders identify patterns of behaviour and of success and failure, applies as much to the corporate tribe as it does to traditional societies.

Most leadership is learned on an apprenticeship model. We learn from experience and observation. When we see someone mess up we quietly make a note not to mess up in the same way: we have plenty of creative ways we can mess up ourselves without copying other people's mistakes. Equally, when we see someone do something well, we are likely to try and copy it or adapt it for ourselves. Over the years we beg, borrow and steal all sorts of leadership DNA from people and places where we have worked. We land up creating our own unique leadership DNA out of all the elements of DNA we have gathered over the years.

The lesson of the wooden leg

Jack was clear: "Our Aboriginal culture is dead, and a good thing too. We should be proud of who we are, not who we were. Young people need to earn respect, get educated and work hard. My father had a wooden leg and that never stopped him from working: I learned from that. God willing, I will never stop work either. Nowadays, too many people are welfare junkies: all their welfare goes on drink, drugs and dice." Jack had started his own community with his bare hands: he had built his first building with 52 telegraph poles, some A-frames and other material abandoned by a local mine. The community now has about fifty people in it, and his children have become a medical doctor, teacher, plumber and electrician. He is rightly proud of them.

Back in town, Brazil was hanging outside the bank hustling change from anyone using the ATM. Everyone called him Brazil because that was the name emblazoned on the dirty green T-shirt that he always wore. When he was not hanging around the bank or the shopping malls, he would sit down with his extended family under the shade of a tree and drink, argue, play cards. His father had done the same and his children were doing the same. The dole seemed to offer no other way of life.

In any organisation, managers are important role models. If you are a mean, miserly, Machiavellian manager, do not expect your followers to be open, kind and generous. Followers look at who succeeds and why they succeed: promotions and bonuses send far more important messages about how to succeed than any formal evaluation system. Be a role model and make sure the right role models succeed you.

There are two problems with learning from experience, bosses, peers and role models:

- It takes a long time, and being old should not be a precondition of leadership in the corporate world
- It is a random walk: bump into good leaders and experience, you advance. Get poor leaders and experience, you find yourself swimming against the tide

The purpose of books and courses is not to provide people with a grand theory, or a course where you start in the morning as a post boy and leave in the afternoon as a charismatic super hero leader. Books and courses can, instead:

- Provide perspectives to refresh, challenge or confirm what you think
- Create a framework for people to learn faster and in a more structured way than they would from waiting for the random walk of experience to take hold

The tribal world is largely unencumbered by books. With little literacy and less money to use or buy books, they have to find another way of developing their leaders. The random walk of the modern apprenticeship system works where you have hundreds of bright eyed graduates coming into your organisation: you can allow competition to sort out the best from the rest. This is

FOLLOWING PAGES
*Libyan Sahara,
pretending to be the
Wild West.*

59

tough on the graduates who progress from bright eyed to steely eyed over a few years. The tribal world cannot afford to waste talent. Each generation needs to learn effectively. The tribal apprenticeship model is simple: the oldest teach the youngest.

A Bambara elder described his life simply: "The first twenty years of my life I was learning. The second twenty years of my life I was doing. The last twenty years of my life I am teaching." As autobiographies go, that has the virtue of simplicity and clarity.

Choidog's story describes not just his own career, but also the career of every successful executive. For a moment, look at how a leader is created the tribal way.

Choidog's story

Choidog, at the age of 74, is the sports superstar of Mongolia. In a horse mad country, he is the top horse trainer and has been recognised by the President as a living national treasure. He had an eventful life. Born in the Communist era, he had to become an accountant. He taught himself the basics by climbing into the yurt (house tent) of an official who had various manuals on accounting and borrowing the texts when no one would notice. He somehow found time to become a wrestling champion: after horses, wrestling is highly prized and it is not by coincidence that one of the great Sumo wrestling champions in Japan, Asashoryu, is Mongolian.

I asked him to draw a map of his life. All he drew from start to finish were horses: nothing else counted. His wrestling days and his struggle to get by with accounting were all irrelevant to him. The only figures that appeared in his life map were his child jockeys, who were family as far as he was concerned.

I asked him how he became a champion horse trainer. He gave three simple answers:

- Horse sense: you have to know your horses
- People sense: the best things always happen with other people
- Hard work: even at the age of 74, he is working all day with his horses

He had, perhaps, given the formula for success in any field:

- Horse sense: you have to learn your trade first, whether it is accounting or athletics
- People sense: leaders never succeed by themselves; leadership is a team sport
- Hard work: successful people are often very driven; they can be uncomfortable to be with as they are often very focused and very driven

Learning horse sense

Most executives start where Choidog started: learning horse sense. Horse sense is the basic trade craft of any horse trainer. When he started out, he learned how to spot a good horse to buy, how to break and train a horse and how to care for horses. At first sight, none of these appear to be very much to do with leadership, but they are the critical foundations on which a leader in his field needs to build. In just the same way, learning how to do stock checks or cut code may not seem to have much to do with leadership, but if you want to become a leader in an accounting or systems firm, it helps to learn the trade craft first.

Some people get so good at their trade that they get stuck as skilled tradesmen. Every organisation is full of these useful people who really know all about the technical aspects of IT, or media buying or the law. They are useful experts, but they are not leaders. To progress towards leadership, they need to learn the next leg of Choidog's leadership formula.

Learning people sense

A nadaam is a festival in Mongolia where all the traditional sports are played: horse racing and wrestling are the main sports. Choidog was given a nadaam in his honour in the middle of the steppe, at least a day's drive away from Ulan Bataar which is the nearest town and the capital of Mongolia. People flocked from miles away for the nadaam. Even a government minister came to bask in the reflected glory of Mongolia's greatest horse trainer. Looking at the map of Choidog's life, the only things that appear are horses and people: everything has been built on those two pillars.

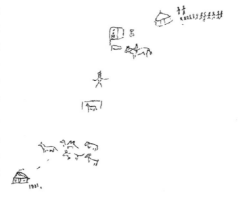

LEFT
Choidog's life map: only horses (and a few jockeys) mattered.

FOLLOWING PAGES
Mongolia, Jalman Meadows.

63

All emerging leaders learn the same lesson. Being a successful technician with great horse sense is not enough. To lead, you need to lead people. That means learning a new set of skills around motivating people, dealing with conflict, coaching, delegating, guiding and directing people as necessary.

Over the decades leaders discover that their trade skills become relatively less important while their people skills become relatively more important. This is the fundamental transition that enables some people to become leaders and means that others get left behind in the leadership race.

Hard work

Choidog had a hard life. He grew up in what was the world's second Communist country (after the USSR). As he grew up he had to balance the requirements of serving the party and being an accountant with his passion for first wrestling and then horses. He was living at least two lives at the same time. At the age of 74 he was still working hard and still riding horses, much to the consternation of his family. There was no question of a work–life balance: his work was his life.

Anyone entering a professional services firm will be familiar with the need for hard work. Ten years of 24/7 will hopefully lead to the gates of Valhalla being opened in the form of admission to partnership. Most emerging leaders discover that there are few shortcuts in acquiring the wisdom, knowledge and experience required to be a successful leader. Many people fail to become leaders simply because they do not have the stamina and determination to get there. Perspiration is at least as important as inspiration on the road to leadership.

❝ *We only excel at what we enjoy* ❞

The real question is how to sustain this level of hard work for a lifetime. Choidog provides the answer again. Watching him at the nadaam it was clear he had a total passion for his horses, his jockeys and the people around him. To him, this was not work. It was fun. He enjoyed what he was doing, so working hard at it did not feel like work. Ultimately, we only excel at what we enjoy. We cannot sustain effort for something we do not care for.

We need to choose our career and our context with care. If we find a place and people where we enjoy work we have a chance of succeeding and leading: even if we do not become the leader, at least the journey will have been a good one.

Conclusions

Many people see leadership as a destination, but you cannot get there without understanding the journey to get to the destination. The tribal recipe for learning to lead has three elements:

- Horse sense: learn your basic tradecraft to start your career
- People sense: learn how to make things happen with and through other people
- Hard work: enjoy what you do so that you can commit yourself to it

These three principles for learning to lead mean that we have to learn through experience and observing others. This means that existing leaders are important as role models: others will learn both good and bad lessons from us. Perhaps our greatest legacy is to create the next generation of leaders who can do better than we have ever done.

LEFT
Taking tea with Chief Kool. There were no cucumber sandwiches. (AW).

5. Skills and Knowledge

From "know what" to "know how": tacit versus explicit knowledge

OPPOSITE
Door of a ger, Mongolia.

There is a romance about the secret knowledge of tribes. The romance ranges from New Age intrigue with their chaminist traditions to the highly commercial pursuit of natural drugs and compounds that tribes have found to cure disease.

All this romance was completely lost on me when the snowmobile went through the ice. Broadly speaking, it is preferable to have a snowmobile above the ice, not below it. The first problem was to realise we could not call road-side assistance to tow us out of trouble: the nearest road was about 50 kilometres away. The second problem was the boot. Dressing for an Arctic winter is an art form involving many layers of different materials. The foot is best encased in a waterproof, rigid plastic outer boot. Inside that there is a felt boot; inside that there are various layers of sock. This keeps feet warm even when you are sleeping outside and the temperature hits −25 degrees Centigrade. The real enemy is not cold: it is damp. If the clothing gets wet, from sweat or anything else, you land up wearing a block of ice about your body. This is not a good idea. If you manage to let your boot go under the ice with the snowmobile, you can look forward to a block of ice at the end of your leg. Eventually, you will have no foot. And a plastic boot keeps water or ice in as effectively as it keeps water out. You therefore have a choice of putting on a wet felt boot that will turn to ice or not wearing any boots and watching your feet turn to ice. This is not a pleasant choice.

At this moment, everything I had learned (or tried to learn) about marketing, finance, accounting, leadership, strategy, change and organisations felt profoundly irrelevant. All that mattered was finding a solution to an icy foot: I could not recall that being taught at business school, but I may have been asleep at the time.

69

Making an arctic boot: easy, if you remembered to bring the dried grass with you.

Lars Matthis, the Saami reindeer herder, has not had the benefit of an expensive MBA, but he knows all about snow, ice, herding reindeer and how to handle all the minor crises that happen in the course of the annual reindeer migration. This is knowledge born of experience. Lars recognised the problem and went to his snowmobile. He pulled out some dried grass cut from his pastures in summer and fashioned a boot liner out of the grass. Dried grass is good insulation and absorbs water well: it is more effective than any high tech Arctic gear you can buy at vast expense in trendy adventure equipment shops. After changing the grass a few times, the foot was dry and warm and the mini drama was over.

Finance and accounting are classic types of explicit knowledge. Explicit knowledge can be written down and transferred through anything from books to corporate knowledge bases. Lars' knowledge is classic tacit knowledge: he has know-how which is pretty difficult to codify in a book and which relies on his experience and skills.

For the most part, traditional societies are long on tacit knowledge (know-how passed from mother to daughter and father to son). Oral tradition is critical to their knowledge. They are weak at explicit knowledge, not least of all because literacy levels are often low so there is not much point in writing everything down.

Progressing through know-how

Progression within the tribe is based mainly on age. From the Dogon to the Maasai, children progress in cohorts that span anything from three to seven years. In the simple words of a Bambara farmer, there are three stages to life: "For twenty years you learn, for twenty years you do and finally you teach the next generation for twenty years."

Most of the skills they acquire would be difficult to write down in a book. You do not learn to ride a horse by reading a book: you have to do it. The nomads say you have not learned to ride until you have learned to fall off: great riders have fallen off many times. After a day in and out of the saddle, I asked if this made me a great rider: they fell strangely silent in reply.

The nomads are master of tacit knowledge, or know-how. They may score very poorly on the knowledge that figures in aptitude tests, and they will probably not do too well in an exam on finance and accounting. The knowledge they need to survive is not just different from the corporate tribe: it is a different sort of knowledge. They need know-how: practical skills that come from

Acquiring a taste for fermented mare's milk

In spring, Mongolia slowly turns from being a white ice desert into an ocean of green grass. In March and April foals are born and their nomad keepers reacquire a taste for fermented mare's milk. A celebration in Mongolia involves large amounts of this vile drink, together with dried cheese from the milk, and a huge fatty sheep's tail. As a guest, you have the honour of indulging in all these delicacies. The politeness of a guest requires that you appreciate the feast. The politeness of the host requires that they ply you with more of these inedible foods, given the appreciation you have just shown.

At least you know where the milk has come from. Outside Choidog's ger (tent home), there were about fifty horses tethered together. When the milk ran low, a small party ran out of the ger to get some more milk. The man's task was to select a mare and hold it steady. The woman's task was to milk the mare as fast as possible, while it swished its tail impatiently in the woman's face. Accompanying the party was a small girl, perhaps no more than six or seven years old. Whenever they found a cooperative mare, which was rare, the mother would let the girl try to do some of the milking. This required patience on the part of both the mare and the mother as the girl struggled with teats, buckets, swishing tails and stamping feet. The girl's delight in achieving some success was mirrored by the mother's delight in seeing her daughter succeed.

The nomads reckon that by the age of ten, a child can do three-quarters of what an adult can do: taking down and putting up the tent, handling horses, milking, making running repairs to equipment and cooking. Only the more physically demanding tasks will be beyond the child, although being a jockey in a horse race is open only to children: as they grow older they grow heavy and slow the horse down. Much to their frustration, they have to retire at the age of thirteen.

BELOW

(left) Milking mares to make fermented mare's milk. (right) Mongolian feast with fatty sheep's tail and fermented mare's milk. Acquired tastes well worth not acquiring.

learning from experience. Business tends to value know-what skills (explicit knowledge), which can be captured in books and knowledge bases, and which can be taught. At least, that is the common perception. Closer examination shows that the most successful members of the corporate tribe do not rely only on explicit skills.

The corporate tribe: know-what and know-how

John is a quietly spoken, highly effective CEO of a financial services firm. He was reflecting on some of the better and worse leaders he had in the organisation and mentioned in passing: "I find I hire most people for their technical skills and fire most for their people skills." He was aghast at what he had just said: it made him sound like a hire and fire sort of leader: in practice he was reflecting the reality of most senior leaders. People get in through the door because of their technical skills and experience: they go out of the revolving door again because of their lack of people skills.

66 I hire most people for their technical skills and fire most for their people skills 99

John had also unwittingly described the career path of many leaders. When people join an organisation, perhaps after university, their first task is to acquire some useful skills that will justify their meagre salaries. They are often shocked to find that secretaries earn more than graduate recruits: the secretaries have more skills and more value to the organisation than a raw recruit, however ambitious the individual may be.

The essential truth that John had revealed was that technical skills are not what make a great leader. People skills make a great leader. Young managers start out by learning technical skills, which can be very dangerous to them. You need to move beyond doing great stock checks for the audit to become a leader. If managers are to progress into becoming leaders, they need to start acquiring great people skills: delegating, coaching, motivating, directing and developing people and teams.

Despite the best efforts of knowledge csars (there was a brief fad for chief knowledge officers), most leadership skills remain like tribal skills. They are tacit knowledge that has to be learned through experience and role models, not from accounting books and marketing texts.

Training and development

Most people are ambivalent about training and development. As a general rule, there is more enthusiasm for training in the "know-what" skills (accounting, finance, law, marketing, etc.) than there is in the "know-how" skills (people management, dealing with conflict and crises, styles of management, etc.). This is human nature. There is no disgrace in saying that you are not a legal or accounting expert, and everyone recognises the value of developing such technical skills, but to go on a course about dealing with people or managing conflict implies that you are no good at dealing with people or conflict. It is a tacit admission of weakness that few people care to admit.

The CIPD (Chartered Institute of Personnel Development) decided to find out why people resisted training. The five most common reasons they found were:

- Too busy at work
- Family or personal commitments
- Insufficient motivation
- Resistance from line managers
- Insufficient culture of learning at work

This needs a little translation:

- Too busy at work (not a priority for me)
- Family or personal commitments (not a priority for me)
- Insufficient motivation (still not a priority for me)
- Resistance from line managers (not a priority for my boss, either)
- Insufficient culture of learning at work (in fact, not a priority for anyone)

People prefer not to learn from courses. They prefer to learn from peers, bosses, role models and experience. This is the natural way of learning. We observe what other people do in real life, in situations we are likely to encounter and learn from what we see. If someone does something really well, we might try to copy it. If they mess up, we make a mental note not to make the same mistake. This is learning in practice, not learning in theory.

Traditional societies do not have much by way of formal training programmes. I never came across the conference centre in the middle of the desert teaching activity based costing for tribes. Tribes may not be good at the theory, but they are very good at the practice. They have to be good at the practice to survive. New members of the tribe are trained and developed at least as intensively as any member of the corporate tribe. The training happens the way that people prefer to learn: from role models and experience.

In Mongolia I found Choimaa, well into her seventies, looking after some of her great grandchildren who were aged between five and eight. She was following the Mongolian tradition that the "oldest look after the youngest". Anyone in between those ages was expected to be outside working with the herds or helping with domestic duties. This mirrors the traditional Bambara life in Mali: twenty years learning, twenty years doing and then twenty years teaching the next generation.

The virtues of the extended family are familiar to any policy maker who bemoans the fate of children bought up by single parents who have to work to make ends meet. Within the close confines of the Mongolian ger, children do more than learn skills such as making felt and looking

*Choimaa, Mongolia.
She had nothing, except
family and happiness.*

after the ger and the herd. They also learn how to behave. They learn the traditions, stories and values of the community. When granny is ill, she cannot be hidden away: the family has to deal with it, and that means that young children help by learning not to shout and annoy granny when she is ill.

Mongolian children learn by doing. They start with simple jobs. A young child might be asked to keep a calf or foal from its mother, so that the mother can be milked by humans. This may seem like exploitation of child labour (and of animals), but the children seem to be having too much fun to realise that they are being exploited by their family. As they master one skill, so they move to more complex jobs like making felt. They are like the apprentices of old. An apprentice painter in the medieval period would start off with menial tasks before even being allowed to take care of any of the master's painting equipment. Eventually, they might be allowed to paint a little background before finally graduating as a master craftsman who could paint the all-important faces in the picture.

This apprenticeship model of learning fits with how executives say they prefer to learn: from bosses, role models and experience instead of books and courses (and certainly not e-learning for most). The challenge for the corporate tribe is to find the balance between the apprenticeship model and the formal training model: both have their places. In practice, they should be woven together.

Training and development for the corporate tribe

Asking sales people to do sales training is an insult to their professional integrity: it implies they do not know their basic job well enough. Yet we knew that their skills may not be uniformly great: some sales people are good at certain sorts of products and clients, others are good at others. There are islands of excellence in a sea of mediocrity: if a way can be found of spreading best practice to the rest, there is a real chance of helping them all improve their results, their bonuses and the company's results.

I decided that being the best nappy salesman in Birmingham did not qualify me to teach them about selling life insurance, so we decided not to teach them at all. We would get them to teach each other. We selected the best salesmen in each category and carefully picked apart exactly what they did well in each sales call. They liked being recognised for their expertise by their peers and managers; they loved being able to pick up other best practices from other sales people. The process appealed to their vanity (recognition) and venality (opportunity to learn from their peers how to sell more). They were able to put their learning into practice immediately, and then bring back more ideas and more best practices for the following month. We had created a virtuous circle of competitive learning and discovery, which had total credibility and practicality because it was driven by them and for them.

We had, accidentally, replicated the tribal way of learning within the corporate tribe. We were creating learning from role models, learning from practice and learning, which is applied immediately.

The role of the trainers was to create the frameworks and processes in which the learning could take place. Used well, frameworks are like scaffolding that people climb up. Used poorly, frameworks become intellectual prisons from which there is no escape: they become substitutes for thinking rather than aids for thinking.

Weaving together a development programme for the corporate tribe is a real challenge. The bog standard training course delivered by a bog standard trainer armed with a flip chart and a franchised theory does not work. The successful programme will have the following characteristics, which mirror much of what happens in traditional societies:

- Learning from peers: this has emotional impact and contextual relevance which formal training programmes struggle to match (see the story above).
- Just in time: put ideas into action fast. The half-life of theory can be measured in weeks, possibly days: unless people get the chance to put ideas into practice, they will forget them and not use them. People learn by doing, not by looking at flip charts and doing a role play. You learn to milk mares by milking them and you learn to motivate people by motivating them.
- Active coaching. Just as Mongolian children are coached and encouraged by their parents, so executives need help and support in putting ideas into practice. The practice is always more

OPPOSITE

Whatever your journey is, enjoy it. Libyan Sahara.

ambiguous, more messy and more uncertain than the theory. That is where a good coach (preferably another executive, not an outsider with a coaching badge of dubious value) can help convert the theory into real learning.

Conclusions

The three principles of learning in the traditional and the corporate tribe are obvious:

- Learn from peers and role models
- Offer training just in time: put ideas into practice immediately
- Coach people actively

These simple principles are often ignored in the corporate tribe where training is seen as a separate activity from work. Training has to move on from the flip chart and role play mentality. Training works when it is linked to action and to coaching, so that people can develop their skills in practice.

With their huge resources, at least relative to the traditional tribe, the corporate tribe should be able to move ahead of traditional societies in three ways:

1. The corporate tribe can call on a huge depth and diversity of experience from inside and outside its own boundaries. This enables it to innovate and adapt far faster and at lower risk than traditional societies which depend on their traditional knowledge.
2. Books and courses create frameworks and structures which, used well, enable people to learn faster from their random walk of experience through different bosses and experiences. Learning can be accelerated dramatically.
3. Explicit knowledge (know-what skills like accounting and law) can be codified and transferred more efficiently through books and courses than it can be by relying on oral tradition and memory.

Some corporate tribes have got the message and do a great job. Many are stuck in the dark ages of training and development.

6. Information Management

Trust the messenger not the message, and never trust a spreadsheet

The information challenge: droughts and floods

Visiting a traditional society is like travelling in a time capsule back to an era our ancestors knew. This is true even when it comes to information management. Our ancestors lived in a world of information deficits; we live in a world of information overload. We will briefly step into our time machine and see what happens to information as we travel back to meet our ancestors.

In the medieval era a monk might spend the best part of a lifetime writing and illuminating a single copy of the Bible. Each word and each page would take time, care and patience. The value of each word was high. The advent of the printing press revolutionised the production of Bibles and helped fuel the Reformation in Europe. By the time movable type was invented, books could be mass produced and a market for nonreligious literature evolved. The twentieth century brought about an unholy marriage between the computer and the photocopier. Instead of creating a paperless office of the future, the computer and the photocopier is drowning the typical office in paper. Electronic words are replicating themselves even faster: with a click of a button, everyone can be copied in on trivial emails and memos on a just-in-case basis.

Information hyper-inflation from an illuminated manuscript to mass e-mailings has done for the word what hyper-inflation did to the German currency after the First World War. Words have gone from being highly valued to being more or less worthless. We have now learned to trust the message only so far as we can trust the messenger. We have travelled from a world of information deficits to information overload: we are drowning in a sea of emails, texts, papers, phone calls and meetings. Even when we go outside to relax, we are bombarded with advertising messages and road signs, from which TV and radio provide little relief.

Traditional societies still live in a world where each word is highly valued. Perhaps because literacy rates are so low, they have high respect for the power of words and information. In Mali, a Bambara elder described how they regarded words: "Words are like gods. With words you can create whole new worlds in people's minds. Words can make people do things. With words alone one man can rule many others. So in our society we treat words with respect. A good speaker will forge each word with the care of a blacksmith, weave them together with the skill of a weaver and will polish them as brightly as a cobbler can. A good speaker says little but means much."

> **" *A good speaker will forge each word with the care of a blacksmith, weave them together with the skill of a weaver and will polish them as brightly as a cobbler can* "**

For the Bambara, less is more when it comes to words and information. For them, quality is better than quantity: this is a message that the corporate road warrior, addicted to email and blackberry, would do well to remember. However, too little information is just as dangerous as too much information. Sir Walter Raleigh only realised that the Spanish were about to invade England with one of the largest fleets assembled in history when he saw the ships arriving off Plymouth. Tribal societies only know that they are being attacked when the attackers suddenly turn up on their doorstep. The Likipia used to put this to their advantage when they went on cattle raiding parties. They never raided the next door neighbours: you do not need a vendetta with your nearest neighbours. They would travel for at least a day and a night to a distant Pokot or Samburu village and strike in the middle of the day when all the warriors were out of the village. This would be a completely unfair fight assisted hugely by the element of surprise. Nowadays, the boot is on the other foot. The Likipia are at risk from marauders with jeeps and guns coming over the border from the largely lawless lands in Southern Somalia. They only know they are under attack when the vehicles arrive and the shooting starts: by then, it is too late.

The challenge for both the traditional and modern corporate tribe is to have the right information at the right time: neither floods of information nor droughts are useful.

Spilling the beans on the market for information

In the highlands of Papua New Guinea, most of the tribes survive on subsistence farming. They eat what they grow and more or less everything they need they either grow or make themselves. Their cash needs are very low by our standards. They will occasionally go to market to buy metal goods, such as cooking pots. They will also buy some clothes. These come from outdoor markets which act as efficient, low cost distribution systems for all the clothes donated by Westerners to their local church and which eventually find their way to Papua New Guinea.

For these modest needs, Chief John and his villagers need some cash. Their only cash crop is coffee. This grows very easily in the rich highland soil. On the way into the village there is a precipitous drop into the river, which is known as "chief fall down". This is where Chief John fell down, spilling his load of coffee beans which he was taking to market. He clearly failed to pick up all the spilled beans, because coffee bushes were happily growing in the ravine where they had fallen.

The problem is getting the right price for the coffee. The good news is that a large market should establish a clearing price in which buyers and sellers are matched at a price that both are happy with: that is the virtue of markets, but it is never that easy. There is only one big buyer of beans, the local coffee factory. The buyers there know that no one who has walked for most of the day with his beans is going to walk the rest of the day back with his beans and no money. He is going to want to sell, and the coffee factory buyer is more or less the only game in town. The villagers have no idea what the world price for coffee futures is doing that day, week, month or year. There is a complete imbalance of information and power between the buyer (the coffee factory) and the seller (the villagers). The factory will win the price negotiation every time.

If the villagers had information about what the true wholesale price of coffee was, and if they knew who other buyers might be, they would get a far better price for their coffee. The right information at the right time has high value.

LEFT
I hope these people are on my side… Highlands of Papua New Guinea (AW).

The tribal world has two ways of managing information effectively. They are equally applicable to the corporate tribe:

- Trust the messenger, not the message
- Less is more: keep it simple

The missing element from this tribal information system is technology: this absence both helps and hinders traditional societies.

Tribal information systems (1): trust the messenger, not the message

The first way of gathering information is to do what tribes and CEOs do naturally: wander around the territory and gossip. The elders in the Dogon village were like the elders in many tribes. They seemed to be hanging around, gossiping and killing the time until time eventually got round to killing them. They were all gossiping by the Togana, the village parliament. The gossip was the normal gossip of village life: who was arguing with who and what should be done about it; young kids misbehaving and what can be done about it; a family in trouble because their crops had failed and what they could do about it. The gossip made sense: this was their way of keeping up to date with what was really happening in the village. Be-

cause they knew each other, they knew what was really meant. One farmer was known for theatricals and would always exaggerate every mini drama, but another was the opposite, if he voiced a mild concern, you could reasonably expect that the sky was about to fall down. The quality and relevance of the information was determined as much by who was speaking as by what they were saying.

They were behaving like typical venture capitalists, who judge a business proposal at least as much on the credibility of the people doing the proposing as on the quality of the proposal. An A grade team with a B grade proposal is likely to do better than a B grade team with an A star proposal: you can improve the quality of the proposal more easily than you can improve the quality of the people.

The Dogon elders were also behaving like an effective CEO. CEOs know that most of the proposals that come to them are not objective. Managers use information in the same way as lawyers: to build their case rather than reveal the truth. CEOs need to hear the truth, not just the pitch. The best way to do this is to wander around, talk to people, watch what is happening and find out what is really going on. Like the Dogon and the venture capitalists, CEOs quickly learn who to trust with information and advice, and who is likely to be more persuasive than accurate in what they claim.

Tribal information systems (2): less is more

Tribes do not have much choice here: they live with information deficits, not information over-loads. At risk of theorising their information systems too far, the tribal community would have a pretty simple balanced scorecard, or peace of mind chart.

The tribal peace of mind chart has four elements:

- Healthy people, skills and culture
- Healthy resources: cattle and goats
- Healthy environment: land and competition
- Healthy future: clear vision

These are essentially the same four things that any leader of the corporate tribe needs to know:

- Healthy people, skills and culture
- Healthy resources: customers and cash
- Healthy environment: market and competition
- Healthy future: clear vision and focus

The details may change in each category, but the four categories are the key to a healthy traditional or corporate tribe. The difference between cattle and cash as the critical resource is not as great as first appears. Capital is derived from the Latin word *capitale*, which can equally mean capital, cattle, possessions and chattels. In ancient times, cattle were capital: they were the walking wealth of the Greeks. To this day, the same is true in Mali, where the Fulani are the nomadic cattle herders of the country. In this role, they act as bankers to the other tribes like the Bambara (farmers) and Bozo (fishermen). When the Bambara or Bozo have surplus cash they buy a cow and the Fulani look after it, until they need to sell the cattle again to raise cash.

There is a solution to the gigabytes of garbage that represents the typical corporate management information system: throw it away. We did this with Steve, who was running a life insurance business. Life insurance is the land of the actuary and spiritual home of useless information. Actuaries are extremely good at being 100% wrong to seven decimal places. This will be understood by anyone who has been wiped out of a final salary pension scheme as a result of actuaries not estimating life expectancy accurately. Steve was groaning under the weight of useless data. We therefore threw it out and started with a single sheet of paper on which he wrote down the information he actually needed to run the business. Steve then got each of his direct reports to produce one sheet of paper which contained what they needed to run their department. The only condition was that their data had to inform the data that Steve needed. This

Mali tribes, clockwise from top left: Fulani, Dogan, Tuareg, Djenne children, Bozo and Bambara.

process was cascaded down through the organisation so that each group at every level built a simple one page dashboard with the information they needed. Even the MIS group found that they were generating less than half the data they actually needed, in addition to a mountain of stuff that was largely redundant. The management dashboards became known as the Peace of Mind (and occasionally "a piece of my mind") charts, after the tribal peace of mind chart with its four simple categories:

- Healthy people, skills and culture
- Healthy resources: cattle and goats (customers and cash)
- Healthy environment: land (market) and competition
- Healthy future: clear vision

Tribal information systems (3): the curious case of technology and spreadsheets

The rock paintings on the cliffs in the Dogon villages and in the Libyan Sahara are the nearest we came to seeing technology used for tribal information systems. The rock paintings encapsulated some of the traditions and beliefs of current and long past civilisations. The drawbacks of not having information technology are clear as soon as you start trying to remember all your appointments and contacts instead of using an electronic organiser (high tech) or diary (low tech).

Information technology can, however, be as dangerous as it is helpful. The Internet has probably done as much harm as good to office productivity: the hours spent trawling the web for personal ends has not enhanced individual productivity at all. If the Internet has been a mixed blessing, then spreadsheets are positively dangerous. The danger with spreadsheets is that people believe them. In practice, most managers know how spreadsheets are constructed: start with the desired answer in the bottom right-hand corner (plus a bit for safety) and then work back up through the spreadsheet adjusting all the assumptions until the right result is achieved. The mathematics may be foolproof, even if the assumptions are foolish. No matter how good the maths are, if the assumptions are bad then the outcome is bad. A spreadsheet does not provide an answer: it provides a starting point for enquiry about the assumptions and the nature of the proposal itself.

❝ The danger with spreadsheets is that people believe them ❞

Tribal societies do not stand the risk of being blinded by technology. The absence of technology forces them back on to the two effective habits that serve them well:

• Trust the messenger, not the message
• Less is more

If the corporate world can apply these two principles to the world of information overload, then technology becomes a powerful support. If information technology is allowed to assume a life all of its own, with consultants racking up ever greater systems integration fees, then everyone suffers.

ABOVE
(left) Ancient rock paintings, Libyan Sahara. An early hunting manual? (right) Establishing identity. The ancient hand will outlast the author's, Libya.

85

Conclusions: back to the future

We are drowning in oceans of information, but information is not a substitute for insight or judgement. At best it is a starting point that tells us where we need to look further. In the search for useful information, the corporate tribe can learn a few successful principles from the traditional tribe:

- Trust the messenger, not the message. Information and ideas are only as good as the people who stand behind them.
- Keep it simple. Detail is a good way of hiding what is important. Focus on what is important first, then worry about the detail if necessary.
- Technology is a support, not a substitute, for information management, judgement and insight.

❝ *Information is not a substitute for insight* **❞**

RIGHT
On the lookout,
Northern Kenya (AW).

7. Culture and Values

Respect for the community: social versus economic capital

Imagine how you would live if you had no money and no savings for the future. You have no access to money in the form of borrowings or welfare payments. Life would feel fairly insecure. If money provides no support and no safety net, you need another safety net: your family and your community.

Business organisations exist to create economic capital. This is the return shareholders expect and employees need and it sustains the business into the future. Individuals in advanced economies are increasingly relying on economic capital instead of social capital: retirement planning requires having a pension plan, not on having children who may, or may not, look after you in old age.

Traditional societies are also focused on the need for survival. For them, survival requires building social capital more than it requires building economic capital. Individuals in a tribe will have little or no money. Their limited economic capital is likely to walk on four legs: the lucky few will have some jewellery or other possessions which can be stored in good times and sold in bad times. When things are bad, individuals in traditional societies rely heavily on other members of the community. Even in good times, there is plenty of social exchange in place of economic exchange: grandparents and the extended family replace the nanny; a house for newlyweds might be built with the help of neighbours. In Mongolia, our hosts were astonished to hear that people pay removal companies money to help in moving house: what are neighbours for, if not for basic courtesies such as helping each other move when the time comes.

Inevitably, both business and tribal organisations find that building only economic capital or only social capital is not enough. Businesses increasingly need to build social capital within and beyond their organisation, while tribes recognise the power of economic capital to protect and enhance their lives. Both sides have much to learn from each other. To discover what each side can learn, we need to venture into both the tribal and the corporate territory. Our first stop on this journey of discovery takes us into the furthest recesses of the corporate tribe.

Anthropology at your desk: discover your tribe's culture

Some traditional societies are a magnet for cultural tourists. Tribal dances, dresses and rituals are photogenic fodder for tourists. Just as the tourists discuss the odd habits of the locals, so the locals discuss the odd habits of the tourists. However, for a real cultural treat, the tourists need look no further than their own office.

Your own office is a cultural jungle which could earn an army of ethnographers their PhDs. You have to follow a wide range of unwritten cultural norms. Failure to read the cultural signals properly can be a serious mistake. The point about these signals is that they do not have a strict functional use in terms of improving profitability. They have a strong signalling function in terms of who we are collectively and where each person is individually within the organisation. Below are a few stereotypes against which to test your own organisation:

Dress codes (formal companies):

- Personal tailors for partners and senior executives
- Brand name designers, off the peg, for middle executives
- Mass retail brands for junior staff

Dress codes by industry:

- Unostentatious suits: government
- Loud and expensive suits: property developers
- Loud glasses, loud shirts and loud mouths: creative industries

Travel rituals, enforced with the help of the airlines:

- Junior executives turn right at the aircraft door
- Middle executives go business – their bankers and consultants go first
- CEO uses the company jet

Pastimes:

- Junior executives drink at a bar and go to a sports club
- Middle executives drink with the Rotary club and play at the golf club
- Senior executives drink at the opera and go to a private island/heli-skiing or other expensive and prestige place which they can later boast about discreetly

In today's world the ultimate luxuries are time and space: cheap stores have displays piled high with merchandise, while expensive boutiques will display a few carefully chosen and expensive items in the window. The same goes with executive rituals. The most senior person gets the privilege of arriving last and leaving first at meetings and conferences. Keeping people waiting is a sign that your time is more important than anyone else's. Even in an open plan office, senior people mysteriously have the most space. Time and space are the privileges of rank in the corporate tribe.

66 Time and space are the privileges of rank in the corporate tribe 99

Beyond the obvious symbols of culture, each organisation has its own informal code of conduct, which is unlikely to be written down anywhere. The code of conduct tells staff how they are expected to behave, for instance:

- How much risk and initiative are we really meant to take?
- How do you get promoted around here?
- Do you challenge dumb decisions or accept them?
- Do customers or profits come first (really)?

Every organisation and department has a culture, whether it is explicit or not. This culture is not the product of the staff manual: it is the result of how people are allowed and encouraged to behave. The promotion system is a wonderful way of signalling what sort of behaviour is valued and rewarded: if getting results is everything, then do not expect the corporate ethics statement to be taken too seriously.

Tribal versus corporate culture: three tests

In many organisations there are some pretty basic expectations which may exist in both the employment contract and the informal psychological contract. These include:

- Respect for the individual
- Pay for performance
- Teamwork

Let us walk through the looking glass into the curious world of the tribe and see how these values translate.

Respect for the individual

This is a basic value of many organisations. Part of this is the quasi-legal obligation around treating people properly regardless of ethnicity, religion, sex or sexuality. It is also about respecting people's private lives and helping them achieve work–life balance in what could be a 24/7 world.

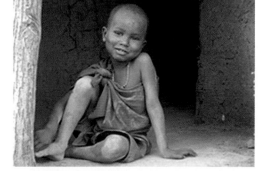

FOLLOWING PAGES
Libyan Sahara.
Beautiful to look at.
Now try living there.

LEFT
Likipia child,
Northern Kenya (AW).

The elder could not believe the talk about "respect for the individual". "What about respect for the community?" he asked. "That is much more important. We cannot survive unless everyone works for the community. In return, the community looks after everyone when they need it. We work for each other, not for ourselves. We have to."

Initiation rites ensure that the price of becoming a full member of the tribe is high. However, the price of not being a member of the tribe is even higher: you become disowned, dispossessed and despatched from the tribe. You have to fend for yourself in a very hostile environment. The realistic alternative is to try to make your luck among the many other dispossessed and desperate in the nearest town or city.

The elder shook his head at the idea of putting the individual ahead of the community. All he could see was divisiveness, politics and competition between people: he was imagining the rat race that many organisations have become.

The respect agenda (1): Dogon territory

The elder sat down in front of the Toguna, which is the village parliament. It has no walls and the ceiling is kept very low: this forces people to remain seated and makes it difficult for fights to break out when the discussions get too heated. He was in expansive mood and decided to set the world to rights. He started in classic form: "The problem with young people today is respect."

My heart sank. I readied myself for a moaning session about how young people need to respect their elders and betters a bit more: it is a universal whine of old men through the ages.

He surprised me when he carried on. "The first problem is that they do not respect themselves. How can they become good people if they do not even respect themselves? We need to help them discover self-respect by letting them achieve challenges and build their own confidence."

"The second problem is lack of respect for each other. They need to be able to earn the respect of their peers, but they don't know how to. They think that respect comes from having what they have: new clothes and things like that. Respect does not come from what you have: it comes from what you do. And if they cannot respect each other, they cannot respect themselves."

"Of course, if they respect themselves and respect each other, they will find it very easy to respect their elders." The elder paused and then laughed. "If we deserve any respect, of course!"

Perhaps the elder had a message which was as applicable to the mean streets of the city as it was to the dusty plains of Dogon territory. He could also have been speaking to many business leaders. Respect does not come from what you have, what you earn or from your stock option package, title or from the trophy house and trophy spouse. Respect comes from what you contribute. Respect is earned, not given. Given respect is shallow; earned respect is deep and lasting.

Thousands of miles away we were in the Australian outback and the respect agenda was evident whoever we talked to. Aboriginal law famously respects the environment: if you let the environment live, the environment will let you live. Less obviously they, are struggling with the respect agenda as a community. Over the last fifty years they have been subject to well meaning government initiatives and hand-outs that have effectively displaced dependence on the environment with dependence on welfare. As with the Dogon, they have realised that respect does not start with demanding respect for the environment, elders or community. It starts by learning to respect yourself. If you cannot respect yourself, it is hard to respect anything else.

The respect agenda (2): Australian outback

Bob put two tea bags and some hot water into his cup, which was an old tin of evaporated milk. He let the bags stew for a good five minutes: he liked his tea seriously strong.

"I used to drink real strong drink," said Bob. "Whiskey, rum. From first thing in the morning to last thing at night. And then there were the drugs, and the arguing and the gambling and the fighting. I was a no-good man. It all went wrong after the guida (white man) started helping us. Before, we had a real hard time, but we had respect. I was sent to a mission school and left it at the age of fourteen. The mission sent me to be a stockman. Got nothing more than clothes, food and shelter for working all day in the saddle. But we had pride, we had respect. The work was hard, but we were good. We lived clean and lived well."

"Then the government said we should get paid proper. So the station (ranch) got rid of all the stockmen and started using helicopters instead to drove the cattle. So we all landed up in town, on dole programmes. Nothing to do all day except dice, drink and the dole. They are still there today. Nothing better to do. They have nothing: they have lost their land, lost their law and lost their language. They have even lost their respect."

"Now I am straight again. We are starting to get title to our land back. Perhaps we can start to get the law back and get some respect back. You have to respect yourself and respect the law."

Many modern organisations focus on respect for the individual. They then wonder why they are not seeing the level of engagement and commitment they desire. However, some high performing organisations still put the group before the individual: the armed forces, churches and many charities are driven more by mission and values than by profit. Respect for the community is only possible when the community is worth respecting. The challenge for many organisations is to help people see that their community, or organisation, means more than just meeting the year end forecast. There needs to be something more to make people put the community first. Think of your own organisation: is it worthwhile in its own right and does it give value and meaning to each member of the community? If it does, you are privileged to be a member of it.

Pay for performance

There are only two problems with pay for performance: "pay" and "performance". As we walked around the village it became very clear that pay for performance was not possible: there was no money. There was no litter in the streets because they had not advanced to that stage of poverty: they were so far outside the cash economy, they had little chance of buying plastic bags and dropping them in the street. You need to be relatively rich to have litter.

Instead of pay for performance, there is recognition for contribution.

Spot the leader

I first met the Bari in a small town in the highlands of Papua New Guinea. They had come dressed in their best clothes for a trip to market: this meant an odd assortment of cast-off T-shirts and jeans, originating in charity drives in America. They wanted to make a good impression in town. One or two of them sported "Tijuana Rock Festival 1986" T-shirts with large pictures of grass (cannabis) on the front. They looked like people I would be very happy to avoid meeting in a dark alley on a dark night.

They all looked pretty menacing, and I had no idea who their leader was. This was not a problem I found when I got back to their village. They got rid of their town clothes and changed into ceremonial dress. It was suddenly very easy to spot the leader. Chief John emerged from a hut wearing traditional Chief's garb, including a huge head dress of Bird of Paradise feathers, which made him look about seven feet tall. I began to feel very underdressed for the occasion.

Chief John gets no pay for being the Chief: no salary, no long term incentive plan, bonuses, accelerated pension contributions, free medical care or re-priced stock options. This would be an interesting plan to produce in the C-suite of the corporate tribe. However, he does get a big head dress, which is a way of recognising him for his contribution to the community.

For Chief John, the feathers are less about recognition and more about contribution. They are a constant reminder that he is there to contribute to the health of the village by resolving disputes, setting direction and being a role model. It is more important that he can give feathers (contribute) than receive feathers.

Some corporate tribes focus heavily on pay for performance. Wholesale financial services, on Wall Street and the City of London, are the classic lands of pay for performance. Extreme performance earns extreme pay. It also generates a culture where someone's worth is measured by their bonus and is reflected in how much they can spend on cars, holidays, homes, entertaining and spouses. A $200 000 bonus would be enough to keep most people happy, but not in this culture. If the person with $200 000 finds a colleague has received $300 000, get ready to see toys getting thrown out of the pram.

Anyone with a super sized income is likely to have a super sized and very fragile ego: being told that someone else is better (because they got a bigger bonus) ensures that they will be looking for a new employer as soon as the bonus cheque has cleared through their bank account. Even in the rational world of pay for performance, pay is ultimately a way of recognising contribution. If it is the only way of recognising contribution, then the organisation faces escalating bonus wars and intense rivalry and politics within the organisation.

Recognition for contribution is a powerful motivator in the modern societies as well as in traditional societies. High performing organisations like the armed forces do very poorly in terms of pay for the degree of risk and discomfort their members have to endure. Instead, they work hard to create a high sense of belonging and recognition for individuals: the rows of medals that veterans wear mean little to civilians but mean a huge amount to their owners. Academic pay is also low: but recognition comes from peers through papers

ABOVE
*My hosts setting off
for the Highlands,
Papua New Guinea.*

published, conferences and ultimately through tenure at a university. At the very apex of success stand the Nobel Prizes: research shows that the winners live on average four years longer than their peers who get nominated but do not win. Recognition is a very powerful force.

In the corporate world, giving medals to staff for successful selling, or photocopying, or taking part in the famous Northern Region campaign of 2008 is probably not going to work. Such awards have no currency in the wider community and would be mocked, but firms can give recognition with currency that is recognised within their community. In running a sales force, I had little discretion over budget, pay rates or bonuses. However, with a limited pot of discretionary money I could run endless small competitions with small (and sometimes not so small) prizes. I gave awards for best salesman of the month, most improved performance and save of the month (for dealing with awkward clients) and awards geared to sales drives on a particular product or account. The value of the award was nothing to do with its monetary value: it was everything to do with the winners being recognised in front of their peers as successful professionals.

Teamwork

Teamwork is a good idea that has been subverted by managers. Teamwork can mean, with different managers:

- "Do exactly what I say or else you are not a team player for me."
- "Help me achieve my goals, but do not be awkward and ask for help in return."
- "Make sure our team beats every other team in the organisation" – popular when it comes to negotiating for a limited pot of budget, bonuses and promotions.

Teamwork is a slightly alien concept in traditional societies. Teams implys that there are different groups within the tribe who compete against each other. Competition within the corporate tribe is vital to success: competition between departments, businesses and teams for a limited pot of management time, money and resource is a highly effective way of making sure limited resources are used as well as possible. This internal competition has a dark side. Competition becomes conflict for resources, while bonus and promotion is the source of much politics and confusion as different teams and managers jockey for promotion. Conflict and confusion are corporate luxuries that the tribal world cannot afford.

Instead of teamwork, the tribal world values commitment to the community. Collective effort is more important than personal success. The role of elders is often to settle the petty disputes that dog any community: broken promises, deals reneged on, misunderstandings, unfair division of effort and personal squabbles. More positively, the tribal community works to support those who need it most.

The alternative tribal value system might look something like this:

Corporate tribe values	Traditional tribal value for the corporate world
Respect for the individual	Respect for the community – for the whole corporate tribe
Pay for performance	Recognition for contribution
Teamwork	Support the whole tribe, not just your silo

These values might appear to be too unworldly for the modern world. They are certainly not easy to put into practice. However, many values-led organisations, from the church to the armed forces, are robust and have stood the test of time. Even in the corporate world, it is possible to put the tribal values into practice.

Tribal culture for the corporate world

Some of the more colourful aspects of tribal culture might not translate easily into the corporate world, although it might be entertaining. Seeing the CEO dressed like Chief John, with a head full of feathers, loin cloth and not much more would at least be slightly more diverting than yet another CEO clone in a business suit. Other cultural values can be translated more easily.

Strong and successful cultures are not the sole preserve of traditional societies. Many corporate tribes can achieve strong and positive cultures. In some ways, the corporate tribe is better placed than the traditional tribe when it comes to creating a strong culture: at least the corporate tribe can decide who they want to become members of the tribe. Traditional societies have no choice about who joins.

Many corporate tribes select people in on the basis of skills, potential and track record. This makes sense. It also misses a vital ingredient: values. Successful corporate tribes will often use values explicitly as a way of selecting people in or out of their organisation. Teach First is a not-for-profit organisation that recruits outstanding graduates to become teachers in challenging schools. By definition, the graduates are not qualified teachers, so it is impossible to select them on the basis of teaching qualifications. One of the essential screens is values: if you have the wrong values in terms of empathy, humility, resilience, integrity and social awareness you are unlikely to survive long in an inner city school. By recruiting to values, Teach First creates a strong *esprit de corps* and recruits people who are most likely to succeed in tough circumstances. Within five years of start-up, it has become a top ten graduate recruiter in the UK, beating many prestigious banks, consulting firms and global corporate organisations which pay much more and have much larger recruiting machines. Values can be a source of very strong competitive advantage, if you know how to use it.

Perhaps an organisation like Teach First seems an exception: it is a not-for-profit organisation so it is inevitably driven by a mission and values. However, the same principles apply in the for-profit world. For a moment, we will take a detour from the outback and the bush and go to an underground station in London. Many of these stations have shoe repair shops. They are small, dark and pretty uninviting places to work. The pay is not great, either. If values have a role to play here, they probably have a role to play anywhere.

From soles to souls

John Timpson, who owns the shoe repair shops that bear his name, found that values are not 'a nice to have' extra: they are fundamental to the success of his business. He discovered that it is best to recruit to values, not to skills. Recruiting good cobblers was never a problem in terms of technical skills: the job of learning how to repair a shoe is relatively straightforward. Recruiting cobblers with good customer skills was nearly impossible: most cobblers related to shoe soles better than they related to human souls.

❝ You can train people how to repair shoes, but you cannot train people to be positive, honest, helpful, attentive and hard working ❞

Eventually, he changed the entire recruiting model: he started recruiting people with good values (honesty and integrity are important in dealing both with customers and all the petty cash), and with good personal and interpersonal skills. It did not matter if they had never seen the sole of a shoe before: he figured you can train people how to repair shoes, but you cannot train people to be positive, honest, helpful, attentive and hard working. As a result, Timpson owns the largest and most successful chain of shoe repair shops in the UK: not glamorous, but it is successful.

Conclusions

Much time is spent and wasted by organisations crafting value statements. These value statements are often so bland that they sound like a United Nations declaration: they are in favour of good things and against bad things. The main problems with such value statements are:

- No one can remember them because they are often too long
- No one believes them because what people do differs from what the values say
- No one can find a way of translating the intended values into action

Traditional societies are not burdened with value statements, complete with the motivational posters and brass plaques. Their values are embedded not in words but in actions. Values are central to the survival of their communities. In the absence of significant economic capital, social capital becomes essential to the health of the community and everyone in it. The focus on economic success can lead quickly to the "greed is good" culture: this can foster high economic performance but sacrifices any semblance of social performance. The challenge for many modern organisations is to build social capital alongside economic capital. Organisations with the strongest social capital (army, church, charities) often have loyal and committed work forces achieving great things on modest salaries.

A good starting point for building social capital is to recognise the values that support a strong social culture:

- Respect for the community
- Recognition for contribution
- Support the whole tribe, not just your silo

Every organisation will create its own unique culture to fit its needs. However, the three most common tribal values would be a good starting point for any high performing organisation.

8. Control and Systems

The lore and the law

At first sight, traditional societies have no systems. They have no computers. They do not sit in cubicle land creating expense reports and trying to surf the web without being detected. They do not have HR departments to put in strategic human capital initiatives or corporate knowledge management systems. They appear to be a complete mess. In practice, however, any society or organisation must have processes and systems to survive.

Traditional societies need control and need systems as much as the corporate tribe needs them. In the absence of technology, their systems are different. More surprisingly, the corporate world can learn from them. The difference between the two approaches can be summarised below:

- Traditional societies: people led and principles based processes
- Corporate tribe: technology led and rules based processes

There are huge advantages to the corporate approach. Technology brings costs down and enables greater depth and detail of control to be achieved. Technology has to be rules based, and rules in turn bring the advantages of predictability and transparency. If the rules are unfair, everyone can see so and they can do something about it, but there is a dark side to the rules and technology based processes. Anyone who has tried to negotiate the arcane world of client service at Microsoft or made a warranty claim on faulty goods will know how technology can be used to block human interaction and how rules become a substitute for judgement. The rules based approach is dehumanising and, if the rules are faulty, not very helpful. Anyone who has been through an airport and played airport striptease recently will recognise the dehumanising nature of a rules based culture (see the box overleaf).

In contrast, traditional communities lack technology. They even lack the paper and the literacy on which to write down all the rules. Instead of rules, they work to principles. These are hugely adaptable to the needs of each particular situation. In a society where everyone knows each other, this flexibility can be a force for good. You can do what is right and fair, instead of dumbly applying rules irrespective of the circumstances. Equally, such flexibility is open to great abuse by leaders who have found power but lost a sense of responsibility. The great kleptocracies of the developing world show how power can be perverted.

Misrule rules the air

Flying used to be a pleasure where individuals were treated like customers. Now it is a painful experience where everyone is treated like a potential terrorist and is harangued by health, security and safety dictators whose main role is to make sure that their employers do not get sued in the case of a disaster. A few examples follow:

1. Airport striptease. The shoe bomber started the rot: he is probably laughing his way through his sentence at the thought of making every air traveller remove their shoes before going through security. If a terrorist attempts to use exploding underwear, airport security will become even more entertaining. Security is clearly important, but seems increasingly to have become a vehicle for crotch grabbers and control freaks to enforce their petty rules such as:

   - Banning nail clippers
   - Putting toothpaste in separate bags
   - Preferring one medium bag to two smaller carry-on bags

   Baggage security getting off the plane is nonexistent: there are no meaningful checks on who picks up which bags. Immigration is, of course, another little paradise for officials and a mini hell for foreign visitors.

2. Get me out of here. Once through security, your health and safety require that emergency exit signs be clearly displayed above emergency exit doors, which sounds very rational. Now think what happens in a fire: most people will be killed by smoke inhalation and the only oxygen left is likely to be at floor level: as you crawl to breath the only air, you will never be able to see the exit signs which are high in the smoke. You will not escape. Fortunately for the airport, your relatives will not be able to sue for negligence because the airport followed the rules about exit signs. But airports know, from practice in aircraft, that there is a better alternative: strips of lighting in the floor to guide you to the nearest exit. This would help you survive, but it is not part of the rules: so you can die instead.

3. Swimming at 35 000 feet. The first time I flew as a child, I wanted to know where the parachute was. Instead, the air stewardess gave me instructions on how to fit a life vest at 35 000 feet. I did not want to go swimming at 35 000 feet. Since then, billions of people have been told how to fit life vests, and precisely no lives have been saved as a result. However, rules are rules, and I still want to know where the parachute is.

Control and compliance

There are at least five levers of control that the corporate tribe typically uses with its staff:

- Information and reporting
- Skills and standards
- Structure and organisation
- Processes and procedures
- Culture and values

For traditional societies, culture and values are the leading form of control. The rites of passage into the adult tribe are high. The worst thing that can happen to a member of the tribe is to be exiled from it: without the tribe, an individual has nothing except the prospect of joining the dispossessed and desperate in the shanty towns and slums of the city. A brief look at how the corporate and traditional tribes use the different control levers illustrates the power of the different methods.

Information and control

The age of hyper-information has become the age of hyper-control. Never have managers been so closely controlled and, by implication, so little trusted. If managers really were trusted by their employers, they would not be controlled through information so closely. This age of mistrust sits uneasily with employers' claims to want entrepreneurial, dynamic leaders throughout their organisation. The corporate tribe is a paradise for the most compulsive control freak: never have managers had so much information at their disposal. Corporate management systems enable managers to put this information to work through the budget, evaluation, assignment, promotion, bonus and disciplinary systems.

Traditional societies cannot consult a computer when they want some information. They have to consult each other. They trust a message as far as they trust the messenger. In this respect, they act exactly like modern day venture capitalists and like many CEOs. They have all grown to distrust spreadsheets. They have played the game of starting with the answer in the bottom right-hand corner of the spreadsheet and then working backwards through the assumptions to arrive at the desired outcome. They know how the result can be fudged. Venture capitalists would rather back a modest plan from someone with a great track record than a brilliant plan from someone who has not delivered in the past.

If traditional societies have an information gap, then modern organisations have a trust gap: trust and information are opposite sides of the same coin. The greater the trust, the less reporting and less information is required. Most of the great empires in history were built with little formal reporting: once the ship left Rome for a distant part of the Empire, then there was not much chance of reporting back on a daily, weekly or even monthly basis. The Empire was built on a cadre of people that Rome could trust to govern in distant places without constant reporting and detailed information. The Empire lasted 400 years, which is more than most business empires can expect.

❝ *Trust and information are opposite sides of the same coin* ❞

FOLLOWING PAGES

Market day, in front of the Mosque at Djenne, Mali.

Skills and standards

Skills and standards have been a way of exerting control from the time of the medieval guilds through to doctors, lawyers, architects and the professions today. Maintaining proficiency is required to maintain professional status. The problem with this sort of control is that it does not cope with change very well. The guilds became closed shops which were more interested in protecting the interests of their members than in innovation or supporting the public good. Latter day guilds, such as lawyers and doctors, show equally great commitment to protecting their members' interests instead of promoting the public interest.

Within modern organisations, structures are often based on skills groups or functional silos. This makes a huge amount of sense because that is how you can build competence and gain focus on core activities. It is also how you land up with silo mentality, inefficient processes and hordes of consultants crawling all over you, mapping your processes and then re-engineering you out of a job. Skills focus helps and hinders in more or less equal proportions.

If organising by skills and standards is awkward for modern organisations, it is even more so for traditional societies. Most people within a tribe are jacks of all trades. They can do everything to a modest degree of proficiency, from tending cattle or crops to building houses. This is good for survival but not good for efficiency: Adam Smith noted the productivity gains to be achieved by specialising in such a trivial task as pin making. By his estimate, a pin maker working alone could produce at most 20 pins a day. Ten pin makers working together, each one specialising in a small part of the task, could make 48 000 pins between them in a day. That is a revolution in productivity. From Adam Smith to Henry Ford's production line is a small intellectual step. This basic level of efficiency has not reached many traditional societies, as the pin makers in Djenne market showed.

Where there is specialisation, it is often based on whole communities. In Mali, there are at least six separate societies that live alongside each other and support each other, each with a specialised skill set. The Bambara are the main farming community; the Bozo are the fishing community along the Niger river; the Tuareg are the traders in the desert; the Fulani are nomadic cattle herders who also act as informal bankers. The towns are distinctively Islamic. As much as each community supports the others, they also engender rivalry in just the same way as functions within a business. Fortunately, consultants have not yet tried re-engineering tribal ways across Mali, although NGOs have a field day trying to impose their ideas locally.

Structure and organisation

The corporate organisation is meant to be a meritocracy: the best people rise to the top. This is healthy for the survival of the organisation but is less healthy for people inside the organisation who find themselves competing hard for a limited number of promotion slots. The tribal world also has a structure that offers much less freedom but much more certainty: there is less opportunity but less conflict. The two most striking aspects of tribal structures are:

- Division of labour by sex
- Division of labour by age

Division of labour by age removes the competitive, political aspect of the corporate organisation. The corporate hierarchy is naturally competitive. As long as there are fewer people at the top than at the bottom, then there will never be enough promotions to satisfy everyone's ambitions. Internal rivalry is constructive for the organisation (it ensures, more or less, that the best talent lands up in the right places). It can also be destructive of individuals in terms of stress, work–life balance and the potential for disappointment.

In tribal societies people progress in cohorts: each cohort might consist of an age group spanning up to five years. Everyone is expected to progress. The cohort approach emphasises cooperation over competition and the importance of the community over the individual. Many societies, such as the Dogon, Bambara and Likipia, boil down to three life stages:

- Learning (children)
- Doing (warriors and farmers)
- Guiding and teaching (elders)

This cannot be replicated directly in modern organisations, but slowly some organisations are taking note of the cohort approach. They are dropping the traditional evaluation system based on a good/bad assessment: such assessments are often poorly received and poorly given. They are also exercises in obfuscation and understatement where the assessor is too embarrassed to give bad news. Instead of the good/bad assessment, they look at skills progression. No one minds being told that they are still developing some skills at their level of the organisation: that encourages a positive and actionable response. Tell the same person that they have bad skills in that area and you get a very negative approach. Focus on building the capability of each individual is more constructive than a school report saying if someone is good or bad at something.

Processes and procedures

As the corporate tribe succeeds and grows, it has increasing need for rules, processes and procedures to replace the dynamic informality of the start-up. At their best, these processes and procedures deliver efficiency, standardisation and quality. At their worst, they encourage crushing conformity and become smokescreens behind which the incompetent can hide.

Indigenous societies do not have employee handbooks or corporate manuals. Instead of a rules based system, they have a principles based system: they do what is right in the circumstances as opposed to following the procedure. Tribal leaders not only have to make the right decision, they have to show that it is a fair decision. For instance, when we visited Chief John's village in the highlands of Papua New Guinea, he had to explain what was going on to the village. He could not copy everyone on an email. Instead, he asked the owners of the one table, the bench and the two chairs in the village to bring them to the main street. We were then allowed to sit on the chairs behind the table. He then stood up and explained to everyone why we were there. Two hours and many questions later, everyone was satisfied and we were greeted fully into the community. This was good news for us, but less good news for the pig which became the centre of the celebrations that evening. This approach to decision making looks inefficient. On balance, however, it is probably best not to gather everyone in the boardroom and kill, roast and eat a pig next time you have a decision to make.

Slowly organisations are rediscovering the benefits of fair process versus rules and procedures. GE initiated the fad for town meetings, where executives meet large groups of staff and explain themselves and answer questions in an open but structured format. Chief John did not realise that his village meeting was, in fact, a highly advanced management technique from one of the world's

most successful businesses. To him, it was not a sophisticated management tool: it was common sense.

When fair process is applied to decision making, the decision can often take ages to make. Anyone who has waded through the Japanese process of nemawashi, or creating consensus before a formal decision is made, knows how frustrating fair process can be.

Equally, anyone who has seen how fast the Japanese can move once the decision is made will recognise the value of gaining the commitment of the whole organisation, rather than relying on authority to impose a decision. Consensual decision making is second nature to traditional societies. If a leader cannot gain the support and consensus of the community then he should not be the leader. Tribal leaders have to earn their respect and support: it does not come with a big title and the keys to the C-suite.

The new business

Lucy lived in Nairobi with her husband Chris and two children. Getting by was not easy at the best of times. Each morning, Chris set off to work with a kiss from Lucy and would return to a kiss. One afternoon Chris never came back. He had been murdered for a mobile phone and fifteen dollars.

Lucy was left with two kids, no job, no insurance, no bread winner, no social security and the rent to pay. She decided to return to a tribe she had met before and start up a small clothing business with them, in the middle of the bush. First, she needed the permission of Chief Daniel and the tribe. We found her, Daniel and about forty elders underneath some trees by the side of a river, discussing the situation. Two unhappy goats formed part of the discussion: they were slaughtered and cooked for all the elders. A lucky few elders got to drink the blood of the goat from a main artery in its neck as it slowly bled to death.

It was not clear what the tribe should do. How would a white woman fit into their community? What about the children? Where would she live? Who would protect her, given all the wild animals that regularly stalked the land? What would happen if the business failed? Even tougher, what happened if it succeeded and what would they do with any profits? Was this the direction the tribe wanted to go in, or should they stick to their traditional ways?

The discussion went round and round for a day and a half. At the end of it, they decided to let her into the community. As soon as the decision was made, a few of them disappeared with Lucy to establish the place where she could live and to start building a house for her. There was no gap between decision and action.

This was highly effective leadership by Chief Daniel. He could have shown strong leadership and made an "executive decision". He knew it was better to let the community make the decision: then there would be a sense of fair process and commitment to the outcome. It would be very easy to move to action with the support of the whole community on what was a potentially controversial decision. By letting the community make the decision (which he wanted) he avoided having endless arguments, resistance and back-tracking from a decision that he could have made himself.

Decisiveness is a virtue in all good leaders. Great leaders help their followers arrive at the right decision themselves: in that way, they build far greater commitment and enthusiasm than they could by making a decision themselves and selling it in road shows, newsletters and emails.

Culture and values

Control through culture and values has worked with some success for the last 2000 years for the Catholic Church and about one billion followers: lasting 2000 years and having a billion customers would be a fair outcome for most of today's businesses. The Church only has five or six levels of hierarchy (on earth) from Pope to people: Pope, cardinals, bishops, priests and people. I have seen businesses with less than 200 people who manage to have six or more layers to their organisation. Indigenous tribes, like the Catholic Church, are very traditional societies. They also rely on culture and values as the primary form of control and compliance. From elaborate initiation principles through endless peer pressure, the ultimate sanction that the tribe can exercise is to banish a member of the tribe.

Corporate tribes typically have weaker, less homogeneous cultures: culture will vary by level (postroom to boardroom) and by function (sales versus engineering versus HR). Leaving the corporate tribe can be a sanction imposed on the individual: often, it will be a decision that the individual takes against the wishes of the corporation. The ties of loyalty and commitment are much weaker in the corporate tribe.

The challenge for many businesses is how to build a better and stronger culture. For the cynics, a strong culture is a good way of getting high performance on the cheap. The evidence from the tribes is that a strong culture is not easy or cheap to achieve, but the tribes give some good clues as to how a strong culture can be created and maintained.

Every tribe has a very strong mission: survival. Modern organisations face the same challenge, but their employees do not share the same mission. If the organisation dies, the employees simply find another job if they are lucky or fall back on their savings and welfare if they are not lucky. The survival imperative is relatively weak for staff. Those organisations that have a very strong, compelling and distinctive mission tend to have strong values as well, such as the church and many voluntary organisations.

The culture and values of each tribe are reinforced by endless ritual. Deaths, marriages, births, graduation to warrior status are all major celebrations that reinforce the culture. They are also reinforced by stories that are told and re-told. For the Aborigines in Australia, the stories are contained in the law. The law consists of a series of artefacts, each of which represents a story and an aspect of the law. Belief in the law is a strong way of reinforcing cultural norms (see the lore of the law in the box below).

Going into the officer's mess of an army regiment is to see and hear tribal cultural values being put into force in a modern context. The pictures on the walls tell of the great battles and great heroes that the present generation should live up to; admission to the officer ranks involves the elaborate rituals of passing out parades; medals celebrate the right sort of behaviours and contributions; and round the mess table the stories reinforce the norms of the regiment.

Business organisations struggle to achieve the same level of cultural control as either tribes or the army. However, employee of the month awards, celebrating successes and recognising the right sorts of behaviour, are all easy steps towards reinforcing the right sort of culture. Perhaps the most important contribution to creating a strong and cohesive culture is to have a mission that everyone believes in: increasing the wealth of shareholders is not a compelling mission for most receptionists.

BELOW

(left) Preparing for warrior initiation: the rest of it is not so painless, Northern Kenya (AW). (right) Dogon dancers.

The lore of the law and the fear of the spear

The tide was in and had converted the West Arm of the Cambridge Gulf from a modest river to a vast lake, about 10 km wide. On the far side of the river lived the Oombulgurri. In the past, moving the law from one side of the river to the other was a major challenge. Male salt water crocodiles have the habit of mistaking small boats for other males, and attacking them to protect their territory. Making a land trip to a fordable part of the river would take a week.

However, even traditional societies move with the times. The Oombulgurri decided to move the law by plane. They carefully wrapped all the artefacts that comprised the law so that the white pilot would not see the law. They chose one of their young men to accompany the law to its next destination.

A five minute hop took the plane, and the law, to Wyndham. The young man decided to stop for a quick beer in town. In the English language "a beer" is an odd grammatical form: it is a plural singular because "a beer" always seems to mean "many beers". Many beers later, he had completely forgotten about the law. A thousand kilometres away, the elders in Broome knew that the law was in trouble: how they knew, no one knows – but they knew. They hastily phoned some elders near Wyndham to pick up the law, protect it and move it to its destination.

The young man from Oombulgurri was in deep trouble. He was invited back to face the music. He chose not to go back. His family did not make him go back, despite the increasingly determined requests from the elders of Oombulgurri. After several years, the elders decided that the young man and his family had missed his chance of redemption: he would be left to the care of the law itself.

A week later, the young man was on a boat in the river. The boat capsized and the young man died. Since then, 18 out of 20 of his family have died in unusual circumstances and everyone knows the remaining two will not last long.

If you don't believe in the lore of the law, you cannot be controlled by it. If you believe it, you will live by it. For those that do not believe in the lore of the law, there is the spear of the law. Bad offenders, like rapists, get speared through their leg in front of their community. The spear goes through their tendons and they are left with a limp for the rest of their lives, which serves as a warning to everyone else. Even if someone does not fear the lore of the law, they fear the spear of the law.

Conclusions

Every society needs control mechanisms to deal with undesirable behaviour, but in every case, prevention is better than cure. It is better to create a culture where people behave the right way than to have sophisticated systems to deal with people who behave the wrong way. Tribes and modern organisations both focus on prevention, but technology and scale drive them in different directions in how they achieve this.

Laikipia dancing does more for community spirit than pizza in front of the TV.

Large corporate tribes need transparent and consistent rules across the organisation. The problem with all rules based organisations is that rules proliferate: each new situation demands a new rule to deal with it. The ever expanding legal and tax codes are witness to this trend. Combine increasing rules with increasingly comprehensive and intrusive information gathering and information management systems, and the result is that we live in an age of mistrust. We have a culture that is drifting more towards a rules based compliance culture, where rules become a substitute for judgement or common sense.

Traditional societies tend to be smaller and have no technology. Law, to the extent it exists, is principles based not rules based. This enables people to focus on what is right, not just what is legal. This means that the performance bar is much higher. Being a good member of the community is not just about doing no wrong: it requires that each member actively contributes. Compliance is not enough: commitment is expected and is role modelled by all the elders. Control through culture is preferred to control through information: this is a higher trust, a more personal and more demanding form of control.

Smaller organisations, where boss and staff know each other, can often achieve high commitment through a strong culture and strong role modelling by the leader. This high trust environment can be exciting and demanding in equal proportions. The challenge for larger organisations is to maintain a similar sense of belonging and commitment, and to avoid becoming imprisoned by the low trust culture of rules, technology and endless reporting.

9. Survival and Success

A journey to the dark side of the tribe

This book does not advocate reverting to a tribal society, although there is an argument that we still are tribal in our dress, loyalties, habits and taste in music, location and pastimes. Putting feathers in your hair and through your nose is not a guarantee of success at your organisation, although it will get you noticed. It may not even buy you wealth or happiness. More mildly, many people choose to swap the corporate life for a different sort of lifestyle. The corporate types will look down on people down-shifting to their vegan farm in Vermont just as much as the vegan farmer in Vermont will look down at the corporate types struggling with their daily stress. Those are simply lifestyle choices.

Both the corporate lifestyle and the tribal lifestyle are package deals: they mix good elements and bad elements and you do not get to pick and mix the best elements of each. You choose the whole package. The corporate lifestyle provides income, some security, a social network and for many people it provides meaning. It also comes at the price of hard work, stress and a challenge to work–life balance.

The tribal package offers a very high sense of belonging and community, which in turn gives a degree of security to everyone in the tribe. This comes at a heavy price in terms of social conformity, lack of freedom or privacy, and in many cases poverty and poor health.

There are two elements to the dark side of the tribe:

- Social costs: the high price of belonging
- Economic costs: the struggle for economic success, which reveals some of the fundamental reasons for economic success of wealthier countries

Before we make too many assumptions about what success looks like, we will pay a visit to Choimaa to find out what she can reveal about success.

OPPOSITE

The joy of looking at your own photo - Kenya.

Choimaa and the meaning of success

The Mongolian steppe is a vast ocean of green in the summer. Navigation is not easy: there are few landmarks from which to take your bearings, and you can travel hundreds of miles without the benefit of tarmac or road signs. The only clues to help are the occasional white dot, looking like a small boat stranded in the middle of the ocean. These white dots are ger, or round tents, which are home to the nomads. They can easily be packed up and transported away on a couple of horse carts in one day.

Gers are very simple, and always arranged in the same way. They always have the door facing the south, so even on an overcast day you can get your bearings. Inside, they all follow the same arrangement, even down to the toothbrushes and flannels which are neatly stored on the left-hand side of the door, at about chest height. As nomads, they live light and travel light. The left-hand side of the ger (west) is the man's side; the right-hand side is the woman's side, which is where the cooking utensils are kept. On the north side is the family shrine, where all the heirlooms and valuables are kept. This is where Choidog, the champion horse trainer, displayed his trophies and pictures of his favourite horses.

It was here that I met Choimaa: she was over 70 years old and wore a broad, toothless grin. She had had a tough life. In the Communist era, she had worked in the mines. She had survived one of the harshest winters in the century, 1958, when most other families lost all their livestock. She had kept some of her livestock alive by moving the newborns into the ger where the humans lived. At the end of the discussion I looked around her sparse ger and asked her if there was anything she wanted or needed.

She looked at me as if I was mad: this is a look that I have got used to from tribal people when I ask dumb questions. "Why would I want anything?" she asked me, beaming her toothless grin. "I have everything I need here, and I am surrounded by my family. This is all I want."

In economic terms, she was below any meaningful poverty line and was an economic failure, but it was not clear how economic success would have helped her. She had acquired all the social capital she could ask for.

The social costs of the tribe

The recruitment interview is a cruel and painful rite of passage into any organisation. The interviewer has all the power, and often takes great delight in seeing how many hoops of verbal fire the interviewee can leap through before being told that their profile does not quite fit the current recruiting needs of the organisation. To make matters worse, the interviewer decides what the rules of the game are going to be, and rarely tells the interviewee what all the rules are. It is a pretty one-sided game, but at least the interviewee has a choice about where to try their luck. If they are unlucky at one place there are plenty of other places where they can submit themselves to the interview ordeal and hope to pass the rite of passage into another organisation.

Once inside the organisation, the more ambitious manager finds life gets even tougher. There are plenty of other talented, hard working (and occasionally duplicitous, scheming and devious) individuals who are all chasing the same limited pot of promotions, bonuses and organisational resources. Managers quickly discover that the real competition is not in the market place: it is sitting

at a desk nearby. The price of surviving and succeeding in many organisations is high. To become a partner at a leading professional services firm (law, consulting, IT) normally requires a ten year exile from anything resembling a decent work–life balance. The social costs of achieving economic success in the business tribe are very high. The main beneficiaries appear to be the burgeoning army of stress counsellors and employment lawyers who feed off such dysfunctionality with glee.

Interviews and initiations

The Dogon, like many traditional societies, have rituals that young men must pass before entering into adulthood. For the Dogon, the blacksmith plays a large part in this ritual.

Each cohort of young men is taken to some rocks above the village. There they are surrounded by rock paintings that represent their families. There is also a painting of a snake which is about 20 metres long.

After much ritual and preparation the boys are then led past the snake to the blacksmith who promptly circumcises them, having warned them that if they cry out the snake will eat them. Even worse, they will not become full members of the Dogon community.

After their meeting with the blacksmith the boys sit on a rock further away. It is permanently stained red with the blood of their healing wounds. Some days later, they take part in a race, where the winner gets the choice of the girls. Then they spend thirty days wandering round the village dressed in nothing more than paint, thereby showing that they have successfully passed the circumcision rite.

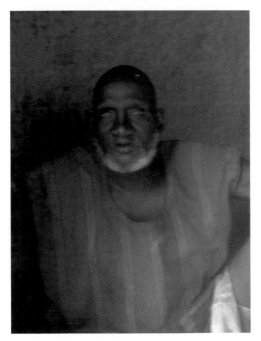

Next time you have to endure the horrors of a job interview, be thankful that you are not being interviewed by the blacksmith and that, if successful, you will not have to spend the first thirty days of your employment wandering round the organisation naked.

The men are lucky compared to the women. The women are subjected to female circumcision: a form of mutilation that would be beyond the comprehension even of medieval torturers in the Tower of London.

Having joined the tribe, you may wonder whether the pain was worth it. Once inside, there is very little choice and even less privacy. The girls tend to get married off early, often to older men to whom they may have been betrothed while still in the womb. Each time a tribal person mapped their life for us, they were able to map both the past and the future. They did not need a crystal ball to see the future. The pattern of life in each community is stable and predictable. You do not get the choice of downshifting, opting out, developing a portfolio or switching careers. Once you are inside, you follow the same path that countless generations before have followed.

Within the tribe, the work–life balance is a nearly meaningless concept. There are work days, rest days and feast days, but all day and every day is a tribal day. They live their organisation 24/7 for 365 days. They cannot escape on holiday or at weekends, while still keeping in touch by Internet and mobile phone. They are not doing a virtual 24/7: they are doing a physical 24/7.

The struggle for economic success

It is easy to dismiss tribal groups as failed societies in economic terms. They are likely to come near the bottom of any tables on wealth and health performance. Yet it is clear that as individuals they are no more or less hard working and intelligent (or lazy and stupid) than their counterparts in the big cities. At least three profound structural differences prevent them from making economic progress. These differences underpin the economic progress of wealthier societies:

- The rule of law
- Education
- Division of labour: specialisation

These things are so obvious that we take them for granted. Living with a tribe is to learn to take nothing for granted. Returning from a tribal visit, the greatest luxury is to rediscover the joys of running water: water on tap that can be drunk without fear of catching a disease, or can be drawn hot for washing, cooking and cleaning. When water has to be drawn from a muddy river and carried in buckets five kilometres through scorching heat, then the idea of clean water from a tap becomes like a vision from paradise.

Instead of taking our economic success for granted, we will look at how these three preconditions for success affect both the traditional societies and ourselves.

The rule of law

It was the cowrie shells that gave the game away: they were the key to the rule of law. Chief John was very proud of his tribal regalia. It consisted mainly of magnificent feathers, from birds of paradise, caught locally in the Highland forest. He also wore some cowrie shells: these came from the coast. For Chief John, this represented progress: such exotic items from far away showed the power of trade. Before the colonial era, such trade was impossible: there was too much intertribal warfare. The advent of colonialism brought a degree of stability that enabled trade to flourish, and its benefits reached deep into the forests and on to Chief John's head dress.

The rule of law is largely taken for granted in Western society: security of contract and respect for property are assumed, and there is outrage when contracts are broken, property is stolen or law on the streets breaks down. Chief John's experience shows what happens when the rule of law is absent: each community has to look after itself, trade becomes impossible and the search for economic progress is replaced by the search for survival.

In many traditional societies, the rule of law remains uncertain and economic progress remains equally uncertain. Returning from Chief John's village to the nearest town involved a full day's walk. This meant going through a neighbouring tribe's land: to ensure the safety of the party 15 villagers went together. This seemed like extravagant precautions, until I recalled the drawings of the children in the village, which recounted burning crops, destroyed houses and cut down coffee bushes. The rule of law did not extend far beyond the highway.

The rule of law did not even extend on to the highway. In town we retreated to the safety of a hotel behind a wall of corrugated iron and barbed wire. Inside we met David, who was dressed in the uniform of Papua New Guinea – second-hand clothes donated to church charity drives in the United States or Europe. David was the local magistrate, and he had just been held up at gunpoint on the road into town. We joked that it was an unwise robber who robbed the local magistrate. David fixed us with his eye: "I will not let this go anywhere near my court. I know which tribe the robbers came from. We will settle this through tribal justice." Even the law personified has an ambivalent view to what the rule of law really is.

This ambivalence towards the rule of law is widespread. Walking through a Dogon village in Mali I heard the eerie cry of an animal in great distress. It was a loud moaning and wailing sound of excruciating pain. They had caught a burglar who had come on motorbike from a village 50 km away. The Chief was not sure what to do with him. If they handed him over to the police, yet another 80 km away, he would be released immediately after a small payment by his family to the police. He thought it would be easier to kill him. In the meantime, they were making sure the burglar regretted his actions.

Tribal justice is like medieval justice in Europe: it is highly personal. The good news is that where victim, villain, judge and jury are all known to each other then a certain amount of fair justice can be administered quickly and humanely. It is also open to huge abuse: get on the wrong side of the big chief, and you are dead meat.

Traditional societies that have subjected themselves fully to the rule of law have also given themselves a greater chance of economic progress. The Saami do not administer their own justice: they rely on the justice systems of Norway and Finland. There are still disputes over land, development, planning and more besides, but there is a predictable and impartial way of resolving these disputes.

Imagine what it would be like if the rule of law was not in force where you live. Like the magistrate in Papua New Guinea, you would find the journey to work a dangerous adventure. At work, you would find it impossible to trade with any other company: even if your goods or services could move across dangerous and hostile territory, you would have little power to enforce the contract and payment with the party at the other end. If you were lucky, disputes would be settled through goodwill or wise intermediaries: if you were unlucky, they would be resolved by force.

The rule of law is a very basic precondition for economic success which we tend to take for granted.

LEFT

Tuareg camel mounted police, Libyan Sahara.

Education

Djenne is a dusty town on a bend in the Niger River. Its big claim to fame is a huge mud mosque, which looks more like a giant mud hedgehog. This is where tribal groups come from afar to trade and to marvel at the sophistication of urban life. In the back streets you can see groups of thirty or forty children squatting in the street while learning the Koran by rote under the instruction of a teacher wielding a big stick.

On the other side of Africa, the Likipia were clear what they wanted from progress: education, health and water, and they wanted them in that order. Even in the driest places, the thirst for education is greater than the thirst for water. In Papua New Guinea, the young Joseph Nomburi saw a missionary with his talking paper, and decided to get an education, even though it meant trekking two days in each direction through hostile territory to get to the boarding school.

It has become a cliché to talk about the war for talent in the global economy. However, when you see the sacrifices being made by the poorest communities to invest in education, you start to see just how highly valued and valuable education is.

Historically, education in traditional societies has depended on oral knowledge passed down through the generations. Oral knowledge is rich enough to make mankind a god among animals: tribal people can make fire, shelter, clothing and food from the land around them. Animals cannot do that but nor can office workers.

The limitations of oral knowledge are painfully obvious to anyone who tries to remember their diary commitments instead of using a diary or an electronic organiser. Managing money in the absence of writing and bank records becomes costly and risky. The entire global supply chain disappears without the ability to write, read, keep records and send messages: we return to being isolated communities relying on our own resources. Without education, we rediscover what it is like to be a traditional society. With education, we have a chance of making economic progress as individuals and as a society.

Specialisation

Adam Smith noted the power of the division of labour in *Wealth of Nations* (1776) when he described the miraculous productivity achieved by pin makers when the job was transferred from one artisan working the whole process to a team where each person executed just one part of the process: "One man draws out the wire, another straights it, a third cuts it, a fourth points it, a fifth grinds it at the top for receiving, the head; to make the head requires two or three distinct operations; to put it on is a peculiar business, to whiten the pins is another; it is even a trade by itself to put them into the paper; and the important business of making a pin is, in this manner, divided into about eighteen distinct operations".

By his estimate, a skilled artisan working alone could make about twenty pins a day. A team of ten semi-skilled workers could make 48 000 pins a day if they were well organised. Adam Smith discovered re-engineering roughly two hundred years before business caught the re-engineering fad.

Specialisation within traditional societies is strictly limited. Each family tends to be self-sufficient: they work their own fields, grow and store their own crops and tend their own livestock. They are the classic jack of all trades, with a range of craft skills that would astonish the average office worker. Equally, tribal people would be astonished by the degree of specialisation that office workers achieve. Think of an employment lawyer advising the HR function of a systems house that provides software to analyse portfolio risk for an investment fund that invests in companies that may or may not make things that tribal people would recognise as useful. We achieve incomparable wealth in an incomprehensible fashion to tribal people.

Traditional societies do little specialisation, but much compartmentalisation. The roles of women and men are highly differentiated; the roles of the young, the middling and the old are distinct and there are significant, and painful, rites of passage from childhood to manhood.

To the extent that the community takes advantage of its collective capability, it is by working together. This is the opposite of specialisation: it is collective labour where neighbours come together to help build a home for some newlyweds. Dogon men work the fields together, in groups of at least ten: this is a throwback to an era when slavers were active in the area and it was dangerous to work alone. Collective effort works wonders for community spirit: it does little to make economic progress. This was a lesson that it took the Soviet Union roughly seventy years to learn before it finally imploded.

To the extent that there is specialisation, it is limited. In many societies, the role of the blacksmith is clearly a key specialisation. In Dogon culture he carries special significance: he is the person who conducts all the circumcisions, and his forge tends to be the centre of village life. People drop by and talk while he works, so he is the person who tends to know all the secrets of the village first, making him an informal confidante and arbitrator. Mali is also unusual in that whole tribes specialise in one activity, just as a modern enterprise will often focus on one area of activity. The Bozo are the river people who both fish and move people and goods up and down the Niger River. The Bambara are the main farming society, and they are settled. The Tuareg are traders, especially north of Timbuktu. The Fulani carry a special place in Mali heritage: they are nomadic cattle herders, which also makes them bankers. When you have spare money, you buy a cow and the Fulani look after it. When you need money, you sell the cow. Meanwhile, you can get on with your own livelihood without having to follow your cow around Mali. This is very limited specialisation compared to the level of specialisation in wealthier countries.

Conclusions

A journey into the dark side of the tribal world leads to a few simple discoveries:

- *Survival versus success.* Tribal groups are highly resilient and know how to survive. However, success is more elusive, given problems with the rule of law, lack of specialisation and poor education. These are basic conditions of success which tend to be taken for granted in developed countries.
- *Every society has a dark side.* Advertisers may promise us perfection and we may search for it and even try to buy it, but we are unlikely ever to find it. Equally, no organisation will ever be perfect. We do not need to find perfection: we need to find what fits and what works in each unique situation. If we find what works, we are at least on the road to success, instead of chasing the impossibility of perfection.
- *Be grateful for what we have.* We take much for granted. Try living for a week without clean hot and cold water from taps, mobile phones, electronic organisers, internet and electricity. It is easy to complain about what is wrong while ignoring so much that is good about our society.
- *Challenge what we do.* We do not need to copy tribal life: we probably do not want to return to such a hard life. However, we can learn from them. Tribes help us challenge many of our

assumptions. Only when we learn to recognise our assumptions and challenge them can we escape the prison of the past. This prison of the past is where we blindly continue doing things because that is what we have always done before. Tribes challenge us to think again about what we do and how we do it: they give us the chance to free ourselves from our assumptions and to escape to a better future.

10. From Bush to Boardroom

Putting bush craft into practice

Take a business leader out of the boardroom and into the bush, or the Arctic or any other tribal land and see how they cope. As a simple exercise we asked some business people to build a Mongolian ger (family tent). This is the sort of thing that Mongolian children can do in an afternoon. The best that can be said of the business people is that they provided wonderful entertainment to the Mongolian nomads who watched their efforts. It was a complete disaster, mitigated only by the fact that the exercise took place in summer. If they had done it in winter they would have soon enough found themselves without shelter as the temperature fell below −20 degrees Centigrade.

With helpful guides, 4 × 4 vehicles, air conditioning and a nice lodge to return to each evening, most business leaders can survive quite well in the wilderness. Back at home they can do quite well with armies of support staff, mobile phones, Internet and the corporate infrastructure to support them. Take away the support infrastructure in the bush or boardroom and most leaders struggle.

If the transition from the boardroom to the bush is tough, we started to wonder whether the reverse journey, from the bush to the boardroom, would be any easier. The journey from the bush to the boardroom started, logically, in the bush. We had been asking the normal dumb questions we always ask:

- What is important to you, what must you protect?
- What makes a good warrior?
- What is your territory?
- What threats do you face?
- What are your hopes for the future?

It is a tribute to the patience and hospitality of traditional societies that they put up with such questions for several days at a stretch. To get past the language barrier and overcome any reticence we often ask local people to draw maps of their territory or their lives. These are richly illuminating. Contrasting examples from Papua New Guinea and Mongolia illustrate the point.

Know your territory: Papua New Guinea

The tribe knew its territory perfectly: the hunting, farming, crocodile areas are all clear. They knew where the threats were from other tribes. One tribe was "so weak, we call them uncle": others they worried about more. In corporate terms it was a good strategy map. They knew where their food sources (customers) were and what they had to do to maintain them. They knew where the competition was and how to deal with them. They knew who and what their critical internal resources were. We wondered whether employees of most businesses would be equally clear about the strategy of their organisation.

Mongolian nomads do not have settled territory, but they still have total clarity about the essentials of survival. Their herd follows the four seasons of the year, each presenting different challenges: 1956 was an *annus horribilis*. The winter and spring were so tough that they had to go to extraordinary lengths to ensure the survival of their herd, including keeping the newborn animals in the ger with the humans. The memory of that year has lasted for over fifty years, and has added to the lore of the nomads: that knowledge makes them stronger and better able to cope with another very bad year. The corporate memory rarely lasts ten years, let alone fifty.

We found three consistent themes in all the maps that were drawn for us:

- *Clarity*: acute awareness of the most important challenges they face and the essential resources they can draw on to deal with those challenges
- *Focus*: intense focus on the basics of survival
- *Alignment*: everyone in the community shared the same perspectives on the important things

The corporate world often struggles to achieve the same three things:

- *Clarity*: many people claim to have the answer, but they are HR, finance, IT sales and operations. All the different geographies and business units are often answering different questions. Having the answer is useless if you do not know what the question is. Traditional societies at least have clarity and agreement about what the basic question, or challenge, is for them.
- *Focus*: I am yet to hear of a CEO who wants less focus in the organisation. The corporate world, like the tribal world, is resource constrained. The corporate world achieves focus through conflict and competition: each department, business and function competes for the same limited pot of management resource, money and time. The tribal world cannot afford the luxury of internal conflict and competition: they achieve focus through consensus.
- *Alignment*: lack of alignment is why so many senior executives are bald: it has caused them to tear their hair out with the frustration of trying to align all the different constituencies so that they are all pulling in the same direction.

In theory, there is plenty that the boardroom can learn from the bush. The practice is trickier: although many boardrooms are tribal in their rituals, actually asking a tribal person to lead a high street bank might not go down too well with the shareholders. The incumbent CEO might not be too thrilled with the idea either. It was William, a Likipia warrior, who showed how we might take the bush to the boardroom. William had patiently been answering questions for a day or two. I then asked him to draw a map of his life. As I pulled out the papers and pens, he said, "I'll map my life, if you map your life." I was suddenly hoist by my own petard, so I drew the map (see the box below). As I drew the map, I realised there was no reason why we should not apply the same medicine to boards of modern organisations.

❝ *Having the answer is useless if you do not know what the question is* **❞**

Island hopping through life

It is easy to feel out of place in a traditional society. We may know how to use a telephone and build a website, but we have no clue how to kill and skin a goat, how to build a hut or how to grow some crops. We may be smart, but we are not smart enough to survive long in the hostile environments where many traditional societies survive. This makes us into very curious beasts in the eyes of many tribes: we are apparently rich, smart and utterly incompetent and useless when it comes to the minor matter of survival. Warrior William decided to examine me to find out how to solve this paradox. He asked me to do what I had asked him to do: draw a map of my life.

Twenty minutes later I found myself talking about my favourite subject: myself. I showed how every episode in my life was like travelling to a new and exciting island where I discovered new and exciting things. I called it "island hopping through life". As I talked, William's eyes bulged with disbelief and his jaw dropped in horror.

"That's not island hopping!" he exclaimed, indignantly "That's tribe hopping! No one can hop between tribes. You must stay loyal to your tribe. They need you and you need them.

You cannot desert them!" A corporate warrior can afford to be a mercenary, picking the best employer at different stages of life. The tribal warrior has no choice: there is only one community to which he can ever belong. The corporate warrior puts self first: the tribal warrior puts community first.

It was with some anxiety that I first asked a group of very senior executives to draw their territory. As the paper and children's colouring pens came out, there was a hush of disbelief. After a few minutes, all that could be heard was the quiet, intense application of pen to paper. Since then, we have submitted several thousand executives to the same treatment in over twenty countries, including several governors of Central Banks. By accident, we had found a very effective way of bringing bush medicine to the boardroom.

When executives map their territory we usually find that:

- They focus on what is important, because they cannot draw detail. This makes a map far more concise and relevant than the normal 200 page PowerPoint presentation.
- They are more honest than usual. Everyone know how to play the PowerPoint, presentation and spreadsheet games to spin the story you want to spin: no one has yet figured out how to abuse children's drawings.
- They are revelations: executives draw maps from their own narrow perspective and can often forget completely about minor details such as customers, revenues or competition. When you then ask them to draw where they are on their customers' map, a challenging and productive conversation often follows.

ISLAND HOPPING THROUGH LIFE

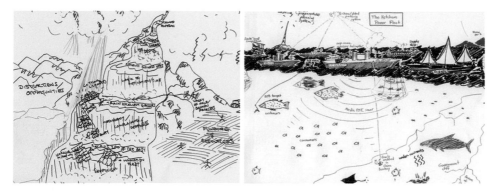

(left) Magic Boat map.
(right) Power Fleet map.

By drawing maps, teams find they can achieve the focus, clarity and alignment that is second nature to tribes, and which is highly elusive in most businesses. Good maps illustrate both the challenges and the way forward (see the Magic Boat and the Power Fleet maps above).

The Magic Boat

Teach First has started successfully. The challenge was how to sustain success. Both the challenge and the way ahead were encapsulated not in a long strategy document but in a simple one page picture, which became known as the Magic Boat. Teach First had started at the bottom of the waterfall. It was enjoying a brief spell in the sunshine as it progressed towards its goal, but it was in danger of being taken off the waterfall by the lure of other goals and by the failure to deliver on its commitments. The message was very simple: stay focused and deliver 100 % of the time. Most corporate strategies can be made that simple, but leaders often feel the need to be sophisticated. Sophistication is the enemy of clarity, focus and simplicity.

❝ *Sophistication is the enemy of clarity, focus and simplicity* ❞

The Power Fleet

The PR agency was growing in China. It faced a familiar problem. When it pitched for new business it would be up against other PR agencies that all had essentially the same PowerPoint presentation saying that they were creative, original and innovative. The challenge was to show that they were creative, original and innovative. Their map proves the point. It carries all the essential messages: we have different tools for big fish (B2B) and small fish (B2C); we have early warning systems to alert you to what is happening in government; our power fleet is hooked up with a global fleet to bring whatever expertise you may need at any time. The visual metaphor is far more effective and memorable than another PowerPoint presentation.

It takes some courage to map your business. It takes even greater courage to map your life. Tribal people find little difficulty in mapping their lives – past, present and future. They do not suffer the modern malaise of a surfeit of choice. With little choice, they have little chance of regretting that they made the wrong choice. In the modern world we can always look at our choices and realise that we could have chosen better: for better or worse we do not get to relive the past.

The clarity of traditional life is captured in the two maps below. The first shows the life of a Bambara farmer: it all revolves around his village and consists of twenty years of learning, twenty years of doing and twenty years of teaching. The only real choice was whether to become a migrant worker for some period within his life. The other life map shows the life of Choidog. I knew from speaking to people who knew him that he had enjoyed an eventful life: under the Communist regime he had to become an accountant to survive and he had also become a wrestling champion (possibly the world's only Communist accountant wrestling champion). Choidog ignored all of this in his map: all that counted for him were his horses. The only people to appear in his life map were his jockeys, who are all children and he treats them as though they were his own. He had achieved extraordinary clarity about what mattered in his life.

Typically, it is much harder for people in developed countries to have such clarity. As an exercise, take twenty minutes to map your life and what is important in it. It is a sobering experience to reduce all your life experience to one page. Do not take too long: this is not a long, deep exercise in psychoanalysis. It is a simple exercise to discover what is most important to you and what choices you have.

> **❝** *Take twenty minutes to map your life and what is important in it. It is a sobering experience to reduce all your life experience to one page* **❞**

RIGHT

(left) Bambara farmer's life map: twenty years learning, twenty years doing, twenty years teaching the next generation, Mali. (right) Choidog's life map: only horses (and a few jockeys) mattered.

Typical of the sort of life maps is the one below from Amanda. It is a map full of life, hope and opportunity. Each petal of the flower represents a different area of life and of opportunity. Within each petal, there are countless further choices and opportunities. This is potentially a very rich life: it is also a life of choice which is beyond comprehension for many people in traditional societies. If we can choose wisely, we will live well. Choose poorly, and we live with regret.

The aim of mapping, and of this book, is not to convert everyone to become tribal warriors. Arguably, anyone who works for an organisation is already a tribal warrior of sorts: you protect territory and subscribe to the rituals and traditions of your organisation just like tribes.

The aim of mapping and the book is to show that we have choices, especially if we have the courage to examine some of our assumptions about our organisations and ourselves. Neither traditional nor modern organisations are perfect, but both can learn from each other. If we learn and make wise choices, then we are more likely to achieve whatever we want to achieve. We stand a chance of controlling our journey and making the most of it. Whatever your journey is, enjoy it.

66 *Whatever your journey is, enjoy it* 99

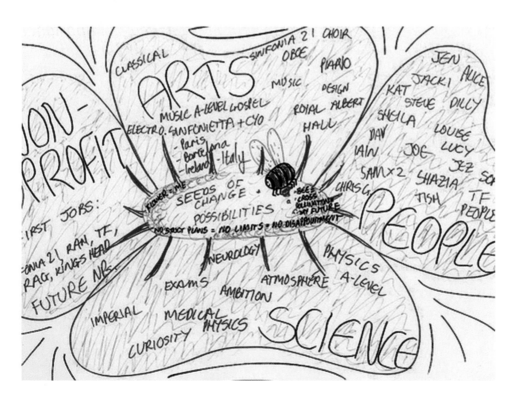

LEFT
Amanda's map.

Journey of discovery.
Heaven or hell?

About the Book and Acknowledgements

This book has the academic respectability of a mouldy cabbage. This puts it well ahead of many academic articles and books on strategy that appear from business schools. Too many leading strategy professors have made their names by coming up with a theory and then retro-fitting a few examples to "prove" their theory, while studiously ignoring the vast army of exceptions that disprove their theory. My lawyers have advised me not to name names unless I wish to discover what tribal poverty really feels like.

If there has been a method to the book, which many will dispute, it has been pretty simple: find a traditional society and hang out with them. While doing so, observe what they do and ask them about it. To probe a little further, we often ask them to draw maps in one of three flavours:

- Map your territory and what is important in it
- Map your life
- Map your year (which is suitable for the nomadic types)

Drawing maps gets round the language problem, is often a source of great amusement for everyone and produces a depth of discussion that is very valuable. We use the mapping technique with businesses as well: people know how to play the PowerPoint and presentation game. They are unfamiliar with the mapping game, so the results tend to be devastatingly honest and insightful: in one day we can make more progress than an army of consultants and analysts can in one month.

The kinder critics would call the above method "ethnography". Less kind critics might usefully stay silent at this point.

Care needs to be taken interpreting what we heard and saw. I try to avoid saying things like "the Dogon do this and the Saami do that". I quickly learned that such generalisations are as accurate as saying things like "all tax officials are nice" or "all Japanese like `hello kitty' dolls" on the basis of one observation of each. I took care to go to two sets of Tuareg (in Mali and in Libya); two sets of Saami (Norway and Finland); and several Dogon, Fulani and Bambara villages. The differences were as notable as the similarities.

All I can claim for this book is "this is what I saw happening in this place at this time". The idea was not to do a comprehensive analysis of each society. It was to find a mirror to look at ourselves. It is, for sure, a distorting mirror because the conditions in which traditional societies survive are radically different from the conditions most businesses find themselves in. Traditional societies have done well at survival and less well at success, which is perhaps the reverse of many businesses.

In retelling stories I have occasionally changed names and disguised places to protect the innocent. It is also possible that I have made some genuine errors in identification or spelling of names: in any event there is always plenty to dispute about how to spell names which traditionally have not been written down by a nonliterate society. Where there are errors, I apologise without reservation.

If the book helps people stop, think and challenge their own assumptions, then it has served its purpose. I hope it has entertained as well. The book does not attempt to give answers, but it does attempt to pose some relevant questions. It lets you draw your own conclusions instead of providing a grand theory of everything.

This book does not suggest that we should all become tribal. There is a dark side to most tribes, just as there is a dark side to every society. I came across practices that would be unacceptable or illegal in the EU or the USA. Female circumcision, or mutilation, is hopefully not part of our future although it is part of the present in some societies today. I took the position that my task was to report, not to change, what was happening: I do not have the courage to be a moral imperialist enforcing my values on to other people.

Language is a problem with a book like this. I have used "tribes" and "traditional societies" interchangeably. The nomads in Mongolia and Norway are not tribal, but writing and reading "traditional society" in every other sentence becomes a mouthful. If I used "tribes" where "traditional society" is perhaps more appropriate, please forgive the poetic licence. Equally, I have used "businesses", "modern organisations" and "corporates" interchangeably. In practice I always mean to refer to "modern organisations" in the widest sense of the phrase: private, public and voluntary sectors can all learn from traditional societies.

Inevitably, the book would not be possible without a veritable army of people who have made it possible. Francesca Warren, my editor at Wiley, showed faith and courage to take on an unusual project: it would not have happened without her. I am more than happy to eat my words about academics when it comes to Dan Denison of IMD, Gerald Ross of McGill University and Nigel

Nicholson of London Business School: they not only have real academic respectability but they also have been inspirational and more than generous with their time in fielding me. Dan believes in real research on culture: check out the Denison survey at www.denisonconsulting.com.

Anthony Willoughby deserves pride of place for being inspirational, for starting off the mapping idea and for introducing me to two tribes. If anyone needs an original, inspiring speaker for an event they could do a lot worse than call Anthony at anthonywilloughby@compuserve.com. Anthony provided many of the best photographs in this book. His photographs are attributed to him. All the other photographs are by the author.

Finding tribes is not always straightforward, unless you are the sort of person who thinks nothing of organising a paragliding expedition over Everest: step forward Nigel Gifford who seems to find no problem making the impossible happen. His High and Wild Group helped me get everywhere from Northern Norway (not sure about sleeping outside in -40 degrees Centigrade temperatures Nigel...) to the middle of nowhere in Australia. If you want real adventure, try www.highandwild.co.uk.

In Mongolia I relied on Jan Wigsten of Nomadic Journeys (www.nomadicjourneys.com). He combines professionalism and a sense of humour, which are essential for survival in such a hostile environment in winter.

I am also grateful to all of those people who have taken part in mapping sessions: they have at least pretended to enjoy and value going back to school to draw their lives, organisations and futures. In particular, I would like to thank Amanda Arney (BBC), Nat Wei (ARK) and Nick Wheeler (Ketchum China) for giving their permission for me to use their maps in this book. For more information on the use of mapping in business you can refer to www.territorymapping. net, while www.leadershippartnership.com gives background on some of the leadership issues touched on in the book.

Last to thank, but first in importance, are the many people in traditional societies around the world who extended the hand of hospitality to me, and put up with some remarkably stupid questions and bizarre requests, such as drawing their entire life on a piece of paper. These are people who restored my faith in humanity, and I hope that they got at least as much out of it as I did.

Index

Note: page numbers in *italics* refer to photographs and figures.

Index compiled by Liz Granger